CREATING YOUR CULINARY CAREER

CREATING YOUR CULINARY CAREER

RONALD HAYES

THE CULINARY INSTITUTE OF AMERICA®

WILEY

Copyright © 2014 by The Culinary Institute of America. All rights reserved.

Photography © 2014 by The Culinary Institute of America.

Cover Design: Maureen Eide

Interior Design: Vertigo Design NYC

The Culinary Institute of America

President	Dr. Tim Ryan '77
Provost	Mark Erickson '77
Associate Vice President — Branch Campuses	Susan Cussen
Director of Publishing	Nathalie Fischer
Editorial Project Manager	Mary Donovan '83
Editorial Assistant	Shelly Malgee '08

Published by John Wiley & Sons, Inc., Hoboken, New Jersey.

Published simultaneously in Canada.

For general information on our other products and services, or technical support, please contact our Customer Care Department within the United States at 800–762–2974, outside the United States at 317–572–3993 or fax 317–572–4002.

Wiley also publishes its books in a variety of electronic formats. Some content that appears in print may not be available in electronic books. For more information about Wiley products, visit our website at www.wiley.com.

LIBRARY OF CONGRESS CATALOGING-IN-PUBLICATION DATA:

Hayes, Ronald J.
Creating your culinary career: the Culinary Institute of America / Ronald Hayes.
p. cm.
Includes index.
ISBN 978-1-118-11684-5 (pbk.)
1. Cooking--Vocational guidance--United States. I. Culinary Institute of America. II. Title.
TX652.4.H39 2013
641.30023'73--dc23
2012001229

PRINTED IN THE UNITED STATES OF AMERICA

V10011027_061419

Contents

FOREWORD

*Y*OUNG CULINARIANS face so many choices as they launch themselves into a career that it can be overwhelming. However, the best way to approach the important task of crafting a solid career trajectory within the culinary arts is to take the longest view possible. This is what I believe makes the power of having significant goals in life so important for all culinarians. Where do you want to find yourself when you are at the height of your career? This vision of yourself in the future acts like a blueprint to move you throughout all the stages of your career.

When you are first entering the field — when you are a novice or apprentice — you may feel that you don't have much control over where you go, whom you work with, or what experiences you will have. At this stage, you are building your skills and learning techniques. A mentor is the person who can help you make the best choices, whether you are just beginning to define your personal career goals, or you are considering getting a basic education at a culinary or management college, or you are determining which applied learning experience best fits your goals.

As you pass through your novice years and become more established — a journeyman — your choices and opportunities may seem to both broaden and become more focused. Here too, the importance of a mentor to help you navigate the waters is crucial. Your career may take a turn from one area of specialization to another, or you may find yourself moving from the hands-on work of the line to positions that put you in a management or even a leadership position. It is critical to take stock of yourself and your skills and to reevaluate your goals once more, and to continue building meaningful relationships with professionals in your field. Decide to deny the acceptance of failure and have faith in the value of teamwork and don't avoid the difficult decisions along the way. Nothing replaces your sense of purpose and determination as you travel along your professional road map.

No one arrives at the status of "master" without having learned a great deal about one's abilities, as well as about the almost unlimited potential that awaits any individual with the dedication and passion that this industry demands. For many, this marks the point in their own careers when they can not only benefit from having a mentor, but they can also grow even more by becoming a mentor to a young culinarian.

Creating a culinary career takes time and effort. That does not mean that there are no guideposts or helping hands along the way. This book offers you the framework you need to dream big dreams, inspires passion, and encourages you to be your best and to be strong in a profession that is ever so rewarding.

Dr. Victor Gielisse, CMC, CHE
Vice President, Advancement and Business Development
The Culinary Institute of America

CREATING YOUR CULINARY CAREER

one

A CULINARY CAREER

BEFORE STARTING YOUR CULINARY CAREER, it is a good idea to take a moment to consider exactly what that might mean. Undertaking a career in the culinary arts means participating in a remarkable history. As Jared Diamond, author of *Guns, Germs, and Steel,* notes, the types and quantities of foods available to various groups throughout history has had a profound influence on the development of society and of various cultures' abilities to grow and advance. Moreover, while we may not have exact records of who first learned to harvest rice and boil it, or who first sampled an oyster, we can be certain that as soon as groups of people gathered into communities, there was cooking going on.

Today, when the culinary arts come under discussion, the picture that first comes to mind is that of a restaurant chef dressed in a white jacket and checkered pants and wearing a toque blanche — the tall, pleated, white chef's hat. There is a tradition of excellence, an aura of authority surrounding anyone rightly referred to as "chef."

It would be hard to describe the "typical" job in the culinary field. In fact, many have taken to using the term *culinarian* to describe the broad scope of jobs this industry now encompasses. In addition, the talented pool of professionals clearly demonstrates that there are plenty of exciting, rewarding, and challenging jobs where you can put your personal strengths to use.

Attributes of a Culinary Professional

Each member of a profession is responsible for the profession's image, whether he or she is a teacher, lawyer, doctor, or culinarian. We take it as a given that someone dedicating themselves to a career in the culinary field is passionate about food and service. Beyond that, however, there are other important attributes.

You will find people who are detail driven and precise, and others who are dynamic problem solvers. Some are great with numbers. Others have a way with people. There is plenty of work for the scientifically minded with a bent for research. People work in for-profit businesses as well as nonprofit. There are individually owned enterprises and international corporations.

Creative individuals may find that occupations such as food writing, food photography, or catering offer the challenges and rewards needed for a stimulating career. There are career tracks for those with a strong corporate or management inclination as well as for those more free-spirited entrepreneurs.

One of the cardinal virtues of any culinary profession is an open and inquiring mind, as well as an appreciation of and dedication to quality wherever it is found and a sense of responsibility. Success also depends on several character traits, some of which are inherent, and some of which are diligently cultivated throughout a career. These include:

- ○ **Commitment to service** *The degree to which a foodservice professional can offer a quality product, as well as thorough customer satisfaction, is the degree to which that professional will succeed in providing excellent service.*

- ○ **Sense of responsibility** *The responsibility of a culinary professional includes respecting not just the customer and his or her needs but also the staff, food, equipment, and facility.*

- ○ **Sound judgment** *The ability to judge what is right and appropriate in each work situation is acquired throughout a lifetime of experience; good judgment is a prerequisite for becoming and remaining a professional.*

At the time that this book went to press, the National Restaurant Association estimated that there were about 13 million people employed in the foodservice industry, and that there would be an additional 1.3 million jobs created by the year 2020. Many of these jobs will fall into some traditional segments, notably hotels and restaurants. However, a great many jobs are to be found in areas that you may not have considered. There are plenty of ways to find a good direction in this field. This quick overview should be just a jumping-off point.

Traditional Restaurants

Auguste Escoffier and César Ritz were directly responsible for making the restaurant an acceptable and even desirable place for everyone, men and women alike, to dine and to be seen. By the time that the Savoy Hotel in London became an acceptable part of life, it had changed forever the way in which the public viewed restaurants. No longer simply stopping places for weary travelers, or clubs for men, restaurants had started on the path to becoming what they are today. Restaurants today run a gamut from fine-dining operations to quick-service or casual chains. The type of cuisine, the style of menu and service, as well as the operating philosophy of the establishment play a crucial role in determining the structure of any specific restaurant.

The size of the kitchen staff can range from one person to a large group, classically known as the "brigade." The size of the kitchen staff is determined equally by the number of meals the restaurant commonly serves and the extensiveness of the menu. The number of people actually employed in a kitchen will vary greatly from one operation to the next. The organization detailed on pages 6–8 is suitable for a very large operation, such as a hotel. In most circumstances, the responsibilities of any given position may be changed to accommodate a smaller staff.

À la Carte Kitchens

In an à la carte kitchen, the staff needs to be able to prepare a wide number of items at any given moment. Adequate *mise en place* (in other words, the basic stocks, sauces, soups, and other foods that are cut, seasoned, and prepared ahead of time so that menu items can be prepared quickly) must be kept on hand. However, the actual preparation of a meal is begun only when an order comes from the dining room into the kitchen, so that all food is cooked to order (at that moment or *à la minute*).

The chef in charge of a kitchen has a wide range of responsibilities. The chef oversees the operation of the entire kitchen, and he or she is ultimately responsible for the food and the service offered by an establishment. To this person falls the responsibility for developing and maintaining the standards of preparation and service of food, in accordance with the practices of the company or facility. The chef develops menus and, where necessary and appropriate, develops and tests recipes to ensure that all menu items are properly and consistently prepared.

Banquet Kitchens

Many large venues count on conventions, meetings, and special events such as weddings, bar mitzvahs, and receptions to generate a large part of their revenue. The banquet staff, from the chef to the servers, is crucial to the success or failure of this part of the operation. A banquet kitchen has pressures that are far different from those found in an à la carte kitchen. In a banquet kitchen, the problem is to feed large numbers of people all at the same time as

Working in a banquet setting

quickly as possible. Foods must be prepared in large batches, as close to service time as possible.

The ability to organize an incredible number of details is paramount. This might include making sure that there are enough tables for a buffet or enough champagne tulips to serve during the intermezzo; hiring or preparing an ice carving; and coordinating with the bakeshop to make sure that the roses on the wedding cake and the linens match the color of the bridesmaids' gowns.

Commissary Kitchens

Commissary kitchens need to produce large quantities of foods and then package them appropriately so that they can withstand transportation and at least some storage time. Then they can be transported to the correct site, where they will be finished close to service time. Commissary kitchens are common in settings such as school foodservice and chain restaurants.

Kitchen Hierarchy

The brigade system was instituted by Escoffier to streamline and simplify work in hotel kitchens. It served to eliminate the chaos and duplication of effort that could result when workers did not have clear-cut responsibilities. Under this system, each position has a station and defined responsibilities. In smaller operations, the classic system is generally abbreviated and responsibilities are organized to make the best use of workspace and talents. A shortage of skilled personnel has also made modifications in the brigade system necessary. The introduction of new equipment has helped to alleviate some of the problems associated with smaller kitchen staffs.

The chef is responsible for all kitchen operations, including ordering, supervision of all stations, and development of menu items. He or she also may be known as the "chef de cuisine" or "executive chef." The sous chef is second in command, answers to the chef, may be responsible for scheduling, and fills in for the chef and assists the station chefs (or line cooks) as necessary. Small operations may not have a sous chef. The range of positions in a classic brigade also includes many others, as follows.

The sauté chef (*saucier*) is responsible for all sautéed items and their sauces. This position is often considered the most demanding, responsible, and glamorous on the line.

The fish chef (*poissonier*) is responsible for fish items, often including fish butchering, and their sauces. This position is sometimes combined with the *saucier* position.

The roast chef (*rôtisseur*) is responsible for all roasted foods and related jus or other sauces.

The **grill chef (*grillardin*)** is responsible for all grilled foods. This position may be combined with that of the *rôtisseur*.

The **fry chef (*friturier*)** is responsible for all fried foods. This position may be combined with the *rôtisseur* position.

The **vegetable chef (*entremetier*)** is responsible for hot appetizers and frequently has responsibility for soups, vegetables, and pastas and other starches. (In a full, traditional brigade system, soups are prepared by the soup station or potager, vegetables by the *legumier*.) This station may also be responsible for egg dishes.

The **roundsman (*tournant*)** or swing cook works as needed throughout the kitchen.

The **cold-foods chef (*garde manger*)**, also known as the "pantry chef," is responsible for preparation of cold foods, including salads, cold appetizers, pâtés, and the like. This is considered a separate category of kitchen work. (For more detailed descriptions of the *garde manger*, see page 11.)

The **pastry chef (*pâtissier*)** is responsible for baked items, pastries, and desserts. The pastry chef frequently supervises a separate kitchen area or a separate shop in larger operations. This position may be further broken down into the following areas of specialization: *confiseur* (prepares candies and petits fours), *boulanger* (prepares unsweetened doughs, as for breads and rolls), *glacier* (prepares frozen and cold desserts), and *décorateur* (prepares showpieces and special cakes). (For more about baking and pastry, see pages 21–26.)

The **expediter or announcer (*aboyeur*)** accepts orders from the dining room and relays them to the various station chefs. This individual is the last person to see the plate before it leaves the kitchen. In some operations, this may be either the chef or the sous chef.

The ***communard*** prepares the meal served to the staff at some point during the shift (also called the "family meal").

The *commis,* **or apprentice,** works under a station chef to learn the function and responsibilities of a specific station on the line.

Cold Foods, Garde Manger, and Banquet Work

In the same way that there are positions on the hot line, and a hierarchy of power, so too are there in the cold kitchen. The areas of responsibility in the cold kitchen are more varied than one might imagine. They include breakfast cookery (eggs, home fries, toasts, cereals, and muffins), cold salads, cold hors d'oeuvre, smoked items, marinated foods, pâtés, and terrines. All of these items are of great importance in most professional kitchens.

Breakfast Cook

A skilled breakfast cook is indispensable in a restaurant, hotel, coffee shop, diner, inn, or bed-and-breakfast. Not so long ago, "eggs any style, choice of bacon or sausage, home fries, juice, and coffee" were all anyone really needed to know about breakfast.

The talented breakfast chef of today must possess the same skills as a sauté cook. The ability to prepare several items at once, with split-second timing, is of paramount importance. Breakfast is generally not as leisurely a meal as dinner or even lunch.

The range of foods that must be prepared for breakfast also calls a number of skills into play. There are hot cereals, eggs in a variety of styles, vegetables, fruit compotes and fruit plates, blintzes, pancakes, crêpes, waffles, muffins, and other breads as well. These are items that, for the most part, need to be prepared as close as possible to service time. Moreover, as Americans become ever more flexible in their understanding of what constitutes breakfast food, the chance for creativity is constantly expanding.

Pantry Cook

The responsibilities of the pantry cook will differ depending upon the type of operation under discussion. In general, however, this station is responsible for preparing a wide range of salads, salad dressings, cold hors d'oeuvre and appetizers, and cold desserts.

If there is no formal banquet kitchen, the pantry cook also may assist the chef in determining what types of foods would be appropriate for a reception or buffet. The challenge to produce attractive, appealing foods while keeping food costs low is one that the truly skilled pantry cook will face repeatedly. For some people, it is like solving an infinitely challenging and constantly changing puzzle.

Butchers and Charcutières

The butcher is responsible for a wide variety of food preparation, and though it is less common to find this as a separate station in all but the largest operations, a well-trained butcher can find a position virtually anywhere in the country, in restaurants as well as with specialty shops or purveyors. Specialty butchering is a skill that is harder and harder to find, while at the same time demand is growing for meats that are trimmed and cut in such a way as to keep them in line with current standards. Locally grown and butchered meats are also in great demand on many menus.

Charcutières prepare a wide array of meat products, including sausages, bacon, hams, and terrines. They are typically involved in all aspects of meat preparation as well as curing, drying, and smoking techniques. This has become an area of great interest as consumers search out locally made, handcrafted foods. *Salumerias* (the Italian name for shops that offer a wide array of cured meats like bacon or prosciutto, sausages, and other specialty meat products) have grown in popularity. Chefs that enter this field are typically driven by an interest in fine-quality foods, as well as a fascination with the science behind how and why foods evolve from their fresh to their cured form.

Obviously, the amount and type of work done by a skilled butcher is varied. However, in many single-unit restaurant operations, there is no butcher. This means that some other position, either the chef or one of the line cooks, will assume this work. On the other hand, it may mean that the restaurant will opt to buy meats and fish already trimmed and cut into portion sizes. The additional cost may be warranted if there is no one with enough skill to perform this work, but the added cost of the meats and fish purchased in this way can be very great indeed.

Garde manger

Garde Manger Chef

The chef in charge of the cold station must be able to prepare a wide range of foods, and often this station will be responsible for the butchering of meats and fish, unless there is a separate butcher station. (Usually it is only very large operations that will have a separate butcher station, as explained previously.)

The garde manger chef has a number of responsibilities, among them to understand which foods are best when prepared in a cold fashion, how and when to marinate foods, how smokers work, what the effect of brining and smoking would be on the food, and how best to arrange and display the items.

Catering and Events

Whenever people gather for several hours, they are going to require food and beverages. At business meetings, coffee, tea, and bottled water — at the very least — are made available for attendees. Celebratory occasions such as weddings, christenings, birthday parties, bar and bat mitzvahs, and anniversaries call for special food and drink to complete the festivities. These are all prime occasions for catering.

From a meal in a prestigious stadium skybox to a mobile lunch wagon on a movie set, catering can be bone china elegant or paper plate casual, but it always means serving good-quality food and drink to many people. Several things distinguish a catering operation from a restaurant.

Catering is usually done by prearranged contract — food and drink provided at a certain cost to a specific number of people. The menu at a catered event is usually more limited than a restaurant menu and is chosen in advance by the client.

The banquet chef must be able to wear a great many hats. He or she will determine what sort of hors d'oeuvre would be appropriate for a reception. He or she also must be able to arrange various styles of buffets, and present the foods in a graceful and appropriate fashion, as well as to determine how best to serve the food, whether that would be by passing the items "butler-style" or by arranging them on a display.

- Excellent organizational skills
- Time management skills
- The ability to multitask
- A friendly, hospitable personality
- The ability to manage stress
- An extensive knowledge of ingredients
- A high level of written and verbal communication skills

- Natural leadership and motivational skills
- A knowledge of social and religious cultures and customs
- Excellent networking skills
- Proficiency in basic accounting principles
- Basic mechanical skills
- Good negotiating skills

Event planners are often involved in several aspects of a function and rely a great deal upon their managerial skills. They may be called upon to interact with the client during planning stages or to arrange additional services beyond those of food and drink, such as photographers or audio-visual supports. They arrange for the staffing of the event as well as any training that their staff may require. In addition, they may arrange for the rental of chairs, tables, linen, china, and all the other necessary accoutrements for the event. They may need to look the site over carefully to determine whether there will be sufficient parking for the guests and the staff. The amount of detail work required to develop a comprehensive list of rental items and a suitable menu is staggering, unless you are extremely organized.

To be a successful caterer, you also need to be able to visualize the entire affair from beginning to end, mentally walking through all the phases of the event. By doing that, you may find that you forgot to order trays or ice tubs for the drinks, beverage napkins, or enough forks to get through the salad course, the entrée, and the dessert. If you are planning to give champagne to 400 people and do not have champagne glasses, the chances of finding someone able to bail you out at the last moment are slim. However, if you rehearse how the party will run, you will raise a champagne glass to give a toast, compare that action against one of your many lists, and realize the problem in time to avert disaster.

There are two main categories of catering:

○ **Institutional** *These caterers at hospitals, universities, airlines, large hotels, and retirement centers provide a wide variety of food and drink to a large number of people on an ongoing basis — usually at the institution itself. The institution typically contracts with a catering company to have this service provided.*

○ **Social** *These caterers provide food and beverage services to civic groups, charities, corporations, businesses, and individuals either on premise at a catering or banquet hall or off premise at a selected location. Hotels and convention centers may have an entire staff devoted to banquets and catering, with the banquet chef heading the kitchen operations and the banquet manager in charge of the sale of the event as well as managing the service and staffing for an event.*

If you think that catering might be a great career option for you, check your skills against the qualities that a successful caterer ought to have (see sidebar). See how you fit in, or find those areas in which you will need more education or help.

Volume Cooking

Cooking for institutions such as school cafeterias, day care centers, airlines, or jails is a career path that many people overlook. The word *institutional* may not have exactly the right connotation for them. Actually, however, working in volume or institutional feeding can be every bit as challenging, creative, and rewarding as working in a white-tablecloth restaurant.

There are distinct advantages to working in volume, contract, or institutional settings. Often, your hours will be regular, and you will very likely not have to work on weekends or holidays. School cafeterias, for instance, usually close during winter, spring, and summer breaks. The opportunity to learn additional skills is readily available; for instance, you may be able to learn about purchasing for large organizations, which could eventually lead to an excellent position as a steward or purchasing agent for a school, hospital, or other institution.

Finally — and this is the advantage that often catches the eye of many people — larger organizations can afford to offer their employees a very appealing benefits package. It may include such things as paid vacations, sick days, personal time, medical and dental insurance, life insurance, and even profit sharing. These benefits are not always possible in smaller operations. If you have a family, look at what the costs would be for life and health insurance if you had to get these things on your own.

Volume feeding is done in a wide range of settings, and the volume can range from a few hundred people to several thousand. Following are some of the avenues open to those pursuing a career in volume or institutional feeding.

Schools, Colleges, and Universities

Most schools have some sort of on-site cafeteria. Larger schools, colleges, and universities may have a variety of foodservice operations on campus, including a traditional cafeteria, a fast-food-style restaurant, a coffee shop, or other options.

Very often, a large organization that handles the foodservice operation of several schools will be in charge. In that case, the managers will have received training from the parent organization. (Sodexho and Aramark are two such organizations that operate nationwide.)

The chef or chef/manager is responsible for developing menus or for implementing the menus that are developed by the company itself. There are usually modifications required, and there is the inevitable need to work with the students who are the ultimate consumers of the food. They will have specific demands and requests as well. The area of the country will play a part, as will the economic profile of the school.

In addition to overseeing the production of the menus, the chef also will be required to schedule the workers. The division of work in the kitchen for a school foodservice operation is much like it would be for any other kitchen. There will be breakfast cooks, pantry (salad) workers, and hot-line cooks who will prepare the food that is served on the cafeteria line. There may be a separate bakeshop as well that prepares a variety of items, including desserts.

Then there is the dish-room staff, the servers who plate up and serve the food on the line, and other maintenance and service staff. Very often, the less skilled jobs are filled by student workers.

Volume cooking

Hospitals

It is a curious phenomenon that institutions dedicated to healing people have such a notoriously poor reputation when it comes to feeding them. The problem in the past may have had to do with the fact that decisions about food were left in the hands of dieticians. These trained professionals certainly know about what foods are best. However, they are seldom skilled at making those foods appealing to someone who may have very little else to look forward to over the course of the day.

The kitchen staff in a hospital will need to work closely with the dieticians and the physicians to make sure that the needs of patients are met. The foods that are prepared and served to patients are a part of the total care that they are receiving, and these foods can have a strong impact on patients' morale.

Assisted Living Centers

Throughout the country, more and more people are moving into assisted-living centers. The level of assistance can vary greatly, but one of the popular features at any facility is foodservice. While the food at these types of places has often been the butt of culinary jokes, the fact is that the centers are starting to fill up with Baby Boomers, who are used to a certain lifestyle. Many of them may already be committed to a healthy lifestyle that includes plenty of good food and exercise. Of course, as they age, their lifestyle often needs to morph a little to deal with the effects of aging, including diseases as well as physical changes that can have an impact on their eating behavior.

Nursing Homes

As people age, they gradually lose their sense of hearing and their sense of sight. However, it is rare for them to lose their sense of smell or their ability to taste and enjoy foods. If hospitals have endured countless jokes about how poor their food is while nursing homes have largely escaped notice, it is probably because comedians, who may have been to a hospital on occasion, have seldom checked into nursing homes for extended stays.

There are various physical ills that can beset the elderly, and these will certainly change the kinds of foods that they are able to eat. If they have no teeth, or only poorly and loosely fitted dentures, foods that require a good firm bite may be out of the question. In addition, if their physical condition calls for a modification of the diet — for instance, controlling the amount of cholesterol or sodium in their food — this will have an effect as well. Still, there is a great deal of opportunity to make sure that the foods prepared and served to residents of nursing homes are wholesome, nutritious, and interesting. In addition, many people may take a special satisfaction in caring for the elderly or invalids.

Armed Forces

A large number of people who have entered the foodservice industry in the private-business sector have done so after learning their skills in the armed forces. Mess halls are not the only dining options, and it is more than possible to learn a great deal about food preparation, even food preparation of the highest caliber, in the armed forces.

The range of work in the armed forces for kitchen personnel is identical to what might be expected in a very large, very well-organized hotel chain. There are executive chefs, chefs, sous chefs, line cooks, pantry cooks, and bakers.

Correctional Centers

City, county, state, and federal prisons have to feed their inmates. They have a responsibility, on a human level, to the prisoners to ensure that their physical needs of clothing, shelter, and food are supplied. They have an equal obligation to the taxpayers who must finance penal institutions to try to keep their efforts within a specified budget.

The challenge for the director of the foodservice operation is to make sure that three wholesome meals are served each day. It is important to learn how to get and use commodity items available through government programs, how to buy in bulk, and how to produce large amounts of food quickly and efficiently. This type of work is not for everyone, but it can be a rewarding job for some.

The Front of the House

Great service requires great service personnel. In an industry devoted to the culinary arts, the professional staff that directly interacts with the guests is critical to the business's success. A great kitchen staff deserves a great dining room staff. For most restaurants, this means having a great dining room manager and a service staff that is constantly learning about the foods they serve.

The front of the house

You may find that your interest in the culinary arts finds its best expression in the front of the house, where you can have more direct contact with the guests. The dining room manager or banquet manager with a culinary background brings a special knowledge to her or his work. This person is often better able to coordinate work with the kitchen to the benefit of all concerned.

Restaurants that pride themselves on their wine lists usually employ a sommelier, who is an expert on wine and wine service. This expertise, married with a well-rounded knowledge of food and the culinary arts, assures that the guests who visit the restaurant have a great array of selections. But, more importantly, it means that the sommelier is able to give each one of his or her service staff the training and information necessary to give each guest service worthy of both the wine and the food.

There is a wide range of different restaurants in the United States today, running the gamut from expensive to family style. The front-of-house work demanded by each type of restaurant will vary, depending in part upon the demands of the clientele and the menu.

Fine Dining, Free Standing

White-tablecloth restaurants generally are considered the upper end of the restaurant ranking system. They are more refined, elegant, and polished than other restaurants. They also offer more upscale service along with menus featuring excellent (and often unusual) foods, wines, and other amenities. They tend to be more expensive for the guests and higher paying for the staff.

The staff in these restaurants is usually highly skilled and has had a significant amount of experience working in hotel and restaurant operations where the food and service is of the highest quality.

Multi-Unit and Chain Restaurants

These restaurants usually have menus that appeal to families because they offer familiar food, salad bars, and low prices. The foods here are very often prepared fully or partially in a commissary, or central kitchen.

While service in these dining rooms may not demand the same level of skill as in a white-tablecloth restaurant, these establishments do offer a management track with the potential for advancement.

Dining Room Hierarchy

Every establishment has its own variation on the classic dining room brigade depending upon the type and price level of the menu, style of service, and physical structure of the restaurant.

The dining room manager (occasionally referred to as the "maître d'") is responsible for the overall management of the dining room: station assignments, public relations, and the physical maintenance of the room itself. In modern bistros or casual restaurants, this position is known as either "dining room manager" or "host."

Depending on the establishment, the headwaiter may have the responsibilities of the manager or host, or he or she may act as the captain of a dining room or of a primary station in the dining room.

The captain (classically known as the "*chef de rang*") is usually in charge of service in a particular station of tables, takes the orders from the guests, and assists the front waiter in serving the food. The captain must have a profound knowledge of food and wine and be able to translate that knowledge into language that is understandable to each guest.

The host or receptionist is the person who greets (and occasionally seats) the guests, takes phone reservations, and looks after the needs of the front desk area. In casual restaurants, this position often replaces all of the previously mentioned positions.

The sommelier (or wine steward) is responsible for the creation of the wine list, the purchasing and storage of wines (maintenance of the wine inventory), the recommendation of wines to guests, and the wine service.

Second in command of the station, the front waiter takes the order from the captain, relays it to the kitchen through the point-of-sale system or with a hand dupe, and serves the food with assistance from the captain. The front waiter often assists the captain in taking some orders, or assists the back waiter in bringing the food from the kitchen. The front waiter's position may not be as glamorous as that of the captain, but the captain relies heavily on the front waiter's efficiency.

The back waiter or food runner (classically known as the "*commis de suite*") brings drinks and food to the front waiter, sets up the guéridon (the cart used for tableside cooking and service) as needed, gets all food and beverage for the assigned station, helps clear, and generally assists the front waiter.

The bus person or "busser" is often an apprentice or trainee to become a back waiter or room service waiter and may work his or her way up the ranks. The bus person is responsible for stocking side stands and guéridons, and for cleaning during the preparation time prior to service. The busser is an extremely valuable member of the service team and can be integral to that team's success. A great busser can lighten the burden on the rest of the service team, enabling them to concentrate more on serving the guests.

Baking and Pastry

Bakers, bakers' assistants, and pastry chefs very often are considered specialists. There was a tendency in the past to divide the kitchen so completely that it was not unusual to have pastry chefs professing total ignorance of what went on in other parts of the kitchen.

Some young chefs turn to baking and pastry after spending some time or getting training in the hot kitchen. They can tell you that they find that the underlying principles are the same. Still, time spent in the hot kitchen is not essential. If you know that the bakeshop is where your talents and interests lie, you should tailor your education and training so that you can get the most benefit out of your time spent in school or as an apprentice.

It is undeniably true that a good chef must be well versed in all areas of the kitchen, including the bakeshop. His or her ability to work with a variety of pastry doughs, mousses, and other mixtures more commonly associated with the bakeshop is a good indicator of the seriousness of his or her commitment to excellence.

However, it is equally true that some people will find that they are more drawn to work in the bakeshop than they are to work in the kitchen. There are a number of differences between life as a pastry chef and life as an executive or head chef. However, there is no difference in the respect to which those who have reached the upper levels of either branch of the culinary arts are entitled.

A quick look through the Yellow Pages, the offerings in your local bookstore, or the word-of-mouth information you may come across will prove not only that bakeshops are still alive, but also that they are gaining in recognition and prestige. Small and not-so-small bakeries are producing some exceptional artisanal breads, using a combination of traditional and modern techniques.

Bakeshops are noted primarily for their production of muffins, quick breads, yeast breads, rolls, and simple desserts. Although this generally is not considered glamorous work, it is work that demands skill, creativity, and the ability to produce large amounts of products quickly and efficiently. Pastry shops generally produce more elaborate baked goods. Some may specialize in wedding cakes, others in items made from puff pastry or croissants. Quick breads, muffins, and other simple batters are relatively easy to prepare, but a bakeshop can make or break its reputation based on their quality.

Bakers must be able to scale (or measure) ingredients accurately, mix them properly, and bake them correctly. This is not just a simple matter of following a formula. On any given day, the air may be more humid, or the flour may be a little harder or drier than the last batch. Only bakers who are skilled enough to see or feel the difference in a dough and make the correct adjustments can ensure consistency. Many large-scale bakeshops use machines to mix and shape doughs, which makes for greater uniformity of product.

Just as there are Certified Executive Chefs and Certified Master Chefs, there are also Certified Master Pastry Chefs. This honor is bestowed on those people who have completed the required and rigorous course of studies and examinations coupled with the appropriate experience.

The Bakeshop

The chain of command in a bakeshop is actually not very different from that of the kitchen. There is a head baker and assistant baker and then as many additional workers as necessary to meet the daily production quota.

The hours for a baker are rigorous, just as they are for most other people working in the culinary arts. Bakers, however, usually start their work before the sun comes up and finish about the time that chefs who work the dinner shift are coming in to work.

The bakeshop

There are bakeshops that do the work from start to finish, and there are those that purchase products that are partially prepared. One bakeshop will have its own "secret" formulas for breads, muffins, and cupcakes. Others will purchase frozen doughs and finish baking them. In either case, the level of expertise required from the workers will determine how well they are paid.

Many hotels and supermarkets, and even some fast-food chains that offer fresh-baked biscuits, will have to do at least some of the baking directly on the premises. While this is often nothing more complicated than adding the required amount of liquid to a prepared mix, others will make more complicated items, such as Danish pastries or doughnuts that require filling, frosting, and glazing.

Fine Pastries and Plated Desserts

Pastry shops are responsible for preparing the more elaborate baked items. These include small French pastries, elaborate cakes, wedding cakes, candies, and other specialty items.

The work that is done in pastry shops is even more exacting than that done in bakeshops. The creations that are produced require a certain sense of form, line, and balance. These are the creations that cause people to stop in their tracks.

Working with chocolate and sugar are among the special skills that pastry chefs must have. These talents take a great deal of time, training, patience, and practice. It is not unusual for a trained chef to decide to move into this demanding and specialized field. Quite often, he or she will elect to continue his or her training, either by attending a school that is dedicated to teaching this craft or by working closely with a respected pastry chef.

Commercial Bakeries

Large bakeries that produce breads, cookies, and other baked goods employ large numbers of bakers. Not all of these bakers need be specially skilled, however. The large batches that are produced are made according to carefully developed formulas. The mixing, kneading, shaping, rising, and baking of bread, for instance, is usually carefully controlled and monitored by sophisticated equipment. Today, it often is computerized to ensure that the quality and consistency of the product is exactly maintained.

However, there is no substitute for humans in some areas, especially when it comes to developing new products. The formulas used for large-quantity production often start as family recipes or new ideas that were unearthed on special trips to Europe or South America. Alternatively, they may be completely new developments.

Then the real work begins. The formula must be continually revised until the product reaches its final stages. At that point, it is ready to go out for test marketing and, finally, full-scale production.

In-House Bakeshops and Pastry Shops

It is often a mark of superior quality if a restaurant can claim, truthfully, that its breads, pastries, and desserts are all prepared from scratch on the premises. Reputations can be made or lost based on the goodness of a piece of cake or other dessert.

It certainly is possible to buy almost anything prepared. Cheesecakes, tortes, pies, and ice creams are all available from purveyors. Today it is even possible to purchase prepared soufflés; all you have to do is bake them in the oven. However, if a restaurant or hotel can afford to offer guests truly fresh muffins, bagels, breads, and other bakery items, the difference is something that even less discriminating customers can appreciate.

Specialty Work and Entrepreneurs

There are stores in most small and large cities that offer specialty items, such as chocolates, éclairs, napoleons, and special cakes, to name just a few. Some shop owners prefer to sell their wares exclusively to restaurants, hotels, and other fine-dining establishments. Others are open to the public.

The production of wedding cakes is one popular area of specialization. This is a very particular type of work, calling for a number of skills and talents. Not all of these talents are strictly related to the actual baking of the cake and mixing of the icing. It also is important to have an artistic sense, the flair to create beautiful things from buttercream, marzipan, chocolate, or royal icing. These ingredients are the special "paints" or "clays" that pastry chefs use to create their works of art.

Many people who do not want to work full-time in a bakeshop prepare cakes, pies, and other items in their homes. They may do this for only one or two restaurants, producing their "signature" items, or they may work with a caterer or catering house to prepare the desserts and pastries for special events. Remember that any business, whether it operates in a dedicated facility or out of one's home, must meet all the requirements for food safety. This includes making sure that all permits, licenses, and inspections are current. Some areas may have specific regulations that pertain to home-run businesses; some may not permit them at all.

*M*anaging a restaurant, or any other business, is a job that requires the ability to handle information, people (human resources), and time effectively. The greater your skills are in managing any of these areas, the greater your potential will be for success.

Managing Information

You may often feel that you can never keep current in all the important areas of your work. Given the sheer volume of information generated each day, you are probably right. The ability to tap into the information resources you need using all types of media is at the heart of managing your operation.

Restaurants, menus, and trends in dining room design have all been dramatically affected by such societal trends as busier, on-the-go lifestyles and increasing interest in world cuisines, as well as such online resources as Facebook and Yelp. Prevailing tastes in politics, art, fashion, movies, and music do have an effect on what people eat and where. The fact that individuals and groups can communicate at lightning speed by virtue of social media means that you can feel the impact almost immediately.

Managing Human Resources

Restaurant operations rely directly on the work and dedication of a number of people, from executives and administrators to line cooks, waitstaff, and maintenance and cleaning staff. No matter how large or small your staff may be, the ability to engage all your workers in a team effort is one of the major factors in determining whether or not you will succeed.

Managing Time

It may seem that no matter how hard you work or how much planning you do, the days are not long enough. Learning new skills so that you can make the best possible use of the time you have certainly ought to be an ongoing part of your career development. If you look over your operation, you will see where time is wasted.

In most operations, the top five time wasters are not having clear priorities for tasks, poor staff training, poor communication, poor organization, and missing or inadequate tools to accomplish tasks.

Food and beverage management

Food and Beverage Manager

This is an important position found in restaurants, both single and multi-unit, as well as hotels, convention centers, and resorts. It can be the goal of both front-of-the-house and back-of-the-house personnel. In order to rise to the rank of manager and succeed at it, individuals must make careful decisions regarding the type of education they will receive and where they will receive it. Managing an operation is a job that requires many talents, including interpersonal skills to handle the tasks of hiring and training staff and dealing with customers, clients, and suppliers. It also requires business skills such as accounting, forecasting, costing, and short- and long-term planning and strategizing. In the past, a great gulf was perceived to exist between chefs and food and beverage managers. However, these days, as more and more people move from the kitchen into management, the overall operation of a hotel or restaurant almost invariably benefits when the manager understands the operation of the kitchen, since it is generally the heart of any food-service establishment.

Graduates with management degrees very often spend some time looking at how the restaurant operation affects overall hospitality operation, but they may not have an innate sense for what is actually possible in a particular kitchen or in a certain type of dining room. As a result, there can be some loss of efficiency. The chef turned manager can offer many skills that someone trained solely in business management cannot; however, there is still a need for experience and mastery of management techniques. That is why many companies and corporations have established "manager-in-training" (MIT) programs to develop those skills and techniques.

As you continue your career, you will move from positions where your technical prowess is your greatest contribution into those where your skills as an executive, an administrator, and a manager are more clearly in demand. This does not mean that your ability to grill, sauté, or roast foods to the exact point of doneness is less important than it was before. It does mean that you will be called on to learn and assume tasks and responsibilities that are more managerial, marking a shift in the evolution of your career.

In an executive position, you must shoulder a large portion of responsibility for the success or failure of your establishment. Executives do not operate in a vacuum, however. Nor do they emerge full-blown one day out of the blue. Even before you wear a jacket embroidered with "Executive Chef," you will have begun to exercise your abilities as an executive.

Learn to use the important tools of your business; budgets, accounting systems, and inventory control systems all play a role. Many organizations, from the largest chains to the smallest one-person catering company, rely upon software systems that allow them to administer a number of areas efficiently: inventory, purchases, losses, sales, profits, food costs, customer complaints, reservations, payroll, schedules, and budgets. If you are not capable of using the appropriate technology to track all this information and more, you cannot be as effective as you need to be.

Research and Development

Many people have exciting jobs working for groups that at first glance might not look like they would employ chefs. These groups include special-interest organizations, research groups, manufacturers, and others.

Everyone who produces a piece of equipment that is used in a kitchen, or a bottled sauce, spice, herb, or mustard, would like to be able to help their potential customer get the most out of their product. This is important in order to build consumer confidence, increase repeat business, and help get

Research and development

them or keep them at the top of the heap. Who better than a chef or someone trained in the culinary arts to help devise recipes, uses, videotapes, booklets, pamphlets, and cookbooks that promote the product?

Other areas that we will look at in this chapter include test kitchens operated by magazines and paid recipe testers who assist in testing the recipes published in cookbooks.

Product Development

When you buy a box of cornmeal and see that there are recipes on the back of the box, do you ever wonder where those recipes come from? When you get a small pamphlet of recipes from a cocoa producer, do you know where those recipes were developed?

There are many organizations, such as the National Avocado Advisory or the Potato Council, that have newsletters or Web sites for the purpose of encouraging chefs or consumers to use certain products. Recipes form a cornerstone of these sites' publications. They act as a blueprint to get the consumer to try the product, whether it is a new and unfamiliar product or an old standard that needs a face-lift.

Equipment Design and Development

Practically every cooking appliance, whether it is large or small, arrives in its box along with a recipe booklet that includes detailed instructions for operating the equipment and producing a variety of dishes using the equipment. The recipes that are included were developed and carefully tested to make sure that the consumer would be able to understand them and make them work.

This type of work can take a good deal of time and effort, but it can be exciting. You will have an opportunity to work with tools that may not yet be available to the public, and the work that is done in research kitchens can have a great impact on the success of the tool's introduction. One need only look at the enormous acceptance that the microwave oven has had to realize that this field is wide open for dedicated workers.

Test Kitchens

Magazines that devote themselves to writing about food often incorporate recipes as well. The person writing about this food needs to have the ability to not only write and do research; he or she also must be able to develop recipes that will showcase the special flavor, texture, color, or nutritional characteristic of a food to its best advantage. This means that the person doing the writing must be able to organize a body of research and put it into a context that the home or professional cook can use.

As there is increasing interest in special foods, such as farm-raised game animals or wild mushrooms, there is increasing demand to know how to choose the best-quality item from among the oftentimes bewildering range of selections. Technological advances also are responsible for increasing the number of options available to the chef and the home cook.

The work done in the test kitchens of magazines can be some of the most fascinating a food writer can find. It combines the best of both worlds: working with food and then writing about it. In many cases, this work also may offer an opportunity to break into the world of food styling and even food photography.

Menu Development

Without some adventurous work in the kitchen and a willingness to try new approaches to food, a restaurant can become "caught in time," and its popularity may wane. Ongoing menu development is essential to keeping a restaurant relevant.

For example, continued work on the part of nutritionists is opening the doors to an onrush of interest in cooking that is based on grains, legumes, fresh vegetables, and fish rather than on the traditional "American" high-protein, high-fat diet. Nutritionists are the catalysts for this new information. But unless and until a chef is available to translate these practical concerns into a meal that satisfies on several levels—taste, satiety, texture, and general appeal—it is not possible for the average chef to make use of these new pieces of information. Instead, he or she will be inclined to stick to the tried-and-true recipes that are sure to please customers.

Other important issues and concerns also play into menu development and have an impact on how successful a restaurant's menu will be, ranging from sustainability to authenticity. Locally and regionally sourced foods are on the minds of many restaurant patrons. The chef must be informed about the issues and also about the potential impact of these concerns on the foods that are purchased and prepared in the restaurant. Research is a factor, as well as the ability to create networks and establish business relationships. Implementing new or revised menu items may also call for additional staff training, even hiring new staff in some cases. There may be a need to develop new standard operating procedures or adjust prices to reflect the new foods or production methods required by the menu. Menu development often has a ripple effect that runs throughout the restaurant, from the advertising and promotion to menu pricing to the style of service that may be required. It may have an effect on kitchen equipment or tabletop and service items.

Corporate Research and Development

Companies that produce food products (General Foods, Pillsbury, and Heinz, for instance) are constantly looking for new items that will capture the interest of the buying public. Before a new cereal, frozen food, cake mix, or salad dressing is introduced, it will undergo exhaustive evaluation and research, not only to determine its potential to make money but also to find out how it acts when it is heated, refrigerated, stored on a shelf, or frozen. In some cases, it may be important to determine how to promote the product to the consumer, whether the consumer is a restaurant or an individual.

Food Communications and Media

There are several careers that involve working directly with food but not actually preparing foods to be eaten by a paying public. Photographers, stylists, and writers are all important to the foodservice industry in a number of ways. They form a central clearinghouse for new ideas, they help establish and demolish trends, and they set the standards by which the public judges what happens in restaurants. There are also fascinating positions in sales and service, public relations, advertising, and media.

Food Photography

Food photography is everywhere you look, from the striking images in food publications such as magazines and books to advertising. Food writers who produce blogs, Web sites, or e-books are becoming increasingly adept at producing good-quality photographs.

While we think of food photography as primarily still images, the emergence of videography for the Web as well as its importance to television programs and films has made this an important medium as well. Some photographers work primarily on editorial jobs such as cookbooks, while others work in a commercial environment to produce the advertisements featured in national media.

When the food is sitting right in front of you, your senses of smell and taste will have an influence on how appealing (or unappealing) it is. You can experience the different textures, the temperature, the thickness, the spiciness — all of the elements that are so important. However, with photography, you can only appeal to the sense of sight. Some foods are not visually appealing. Nevertheless, the challenge is somehow to make them look that way, whether for an ad campaign, a feature story in a magazine, or the jacket of a new cookbook. Trends in photography and video are constantly changing, as is the technology that supports this type of work.

It is important to understand the basic principles of photography and lighting, how to operate a camera, and how to arrange foods so that they look appealing. The ability to work in a digital environment, including being skilled at various types of software and applications, is critical. (For more information and resources related to food photography, see page 247.)

Food Styling

The preparation of the food being photographed and the way it is placed or arranged is often the work of a second person, known as a "food stylist." When you look at a magazine article and are struck by the way the food is spread out on a plate or the way it is garnished or the presence or lack of other items in the photograph, you are usually reacting to the work of the food stylist. They, too, like food photographers, undergo primarily on-the-job training.

Food photography and food styling

While you can pursue a degree in photography or film, you may find that an education in hands-on food styling is only available by means of internships or apprenticeships with established stylists.

It is up to the stylist to make sure that the lettuce leaves are perfect, with not a single detectable fault, and that the sauce is carefully ladled onto the plate after the chicken is arranged to achieve the greatest visual impact.

Without some knowledge of food — how to select the best product and apply the right technique, how to cut the vegetables and slice the turkey — the stylist would be at a loss. (For more information and resources related to food styling, see page 261.)

Food Writing and Communications

All you have to do is walk into any bookstore or do a simple search on the Internet to see that there is a large and seemingly inexhaustible market for all things culinary. Food publications range from single-subject books and blogs on anything from beans to chocolate to those that center on a particular type of cuisine or ethnic style. Some are encyclopedic in their scope.

The people who write the blogs or books, edit recipes, or acquire projects for publishing houses have to have a good basic knowledge of food and cooking in order to be successful and make a living.

Restaurant critics are as important to restaurants as are the people who will dine in them. It is certainly true that critics are notorious for their highly personalized opinions, but it is interesting to note just how influential some critics can be, even in the era of such community-based sites as Yelp.

Food historians and ethnographers help us to understand the current state of the culinary arts by digging deeper into the traditions and history of our culinary behaviors.

Today, writers with a particular slant on the food industry, whether they be concerned with sustainability or authenticity, nutrition or food security, are finding a growing audience for their work, especially if they have a solid grounding in what constitutes both good food and good cooking.

There are a number of trade and consumer publications (both traditional print publications and online resources) that focus on food, and many newspapers devote a portion of their papers (usually on Wednesdays) to food and entertainment. The person who writes these articles is usually well-read in the culinary arts and proficient in the kitchen as well. The kinds of articles that might be called for could range from a simple discussion of how to brew a pot of tea to an informational piece on nutritional cooking or special new foods.

Reviews of cookbooks, small pieces on new foods or equipment, human interest stories, press releases — all of these are examples of the kinds of pieces that you may be able to pitch to magazines to start your portfolio. Read the publications, both trade and consumer, to see what their audience is like. There are special publications that will explain how to submit articles to magazines for consideration. (For more information and resources related to food writing and communication, see page 247.)

Public Relations and Advertising

The number of companies that produce or sell food items or equipment for preparing foods, national councils that promote a particular food, and other special-interest groups that are directly or indirectly related to the culinary arts is staggering. Who would have imagined a National Onion Association? Nevertheless, there is such an organization, and countless others devoted to products ranging from raisins to avocados to potatoes. Some have been around for a long time, like the National Dairy Council, while others, like the Popcorn Board, are relatively new.

What they all have in common is that they need people to help them get their message out to the public. This may mean that they need writers, photographers and stylists, and recipe developers who can all showcase their product or equipment.

There also are numerous advertising agencies, some of which handle food and food-related clients exclusively. The campaigns that these companies devise for their clients are often incredibly innovative and exciting. Someone who knows about food can play a significant role in getting them off the ground, from helping to develop the original concept to getting the food onto the plate and into the photo.

It may be helpful to take additional courses in marketing and advertising in order to qualify for the jobs that really appeal to you, but experience on the job is something that is worth its weight in gold.

Sales

As cooking styles around the world open up to embrace global influences, chefs are looking for a whole bevy of new products such as ingredients, tools, and serving pieces to keep their menus lively and their bottom lines healthy. Skilled salespeople are needed to pitch these products to the end consumers, and someone trained with a background in the foodservice industry has a distinct advantage. Whether you work for a large purveyor or you are a sales force of one for your artisanal cheeses, you have a base of knowledge that can give you an edge. For instance, you would never show up at 12:30 P.M. on a Tuesday if the restaurant is most famous for its lunches. Sales jobs demand great communication skills, especially verbal communication in a one-on-one setting. Organization, attention to detail, punctuality, and honesty are also found on the résumé of the skilled and successful salesperson. Many sales jobs are based upon a commission rather than a straight salary, so your abilities as a salesperson will have a direct relationship to your earning potential.

Summary

In this chapter, we have briefly examined a variety of career possibilities, all related to food. A passion to work with food no longer limits your career options to working long hours in a hot kitchen. Passion alone, however, will not qualify you for your dream job. Creating your culinary career involves active career management: learning and perfecting the skills needed to do the job you seek, creating lasting and active connections with those who can assist you along the way, and crafting marketing strategies that will encourage potential employers to want to hire you. The chapters that follow provide you with tools that you can use to actively define, design, and pursue your culinary career.

Your career is a living, changing entity that requires constant monitoring, upkeep, and adjustments. This book is a resource to assist you at all stages of your career, from building a foundation through achieving a pinnacle position, along with all the stops and starts, twists, and turns that may happen in between. We encourage you to write in this book. Let it be an active part of your career: your log, your journal, your tool of reflection as you create your culinary career.

two

GOAL-SETTING FOR YOUR CULINARY CAREER

NOW THAT YOU HAVE AN OVERVIEW of the enormous amount of variety and potential choices that fall under the umbrella of culinary careers, we turn our focus toward creating goals to help you move toward your dream job by creating logical steps that take you from where you are to where you want to be. Let's divide career goals into short-term (attainable within one to five years), intermediate (attainable within five to ten years), and long-term (attainable in ten years and beyond) and discuss how to create specific tasks meant to bring you to the realization of those goals.

Goal-Setting

"Begin with the end in mind."

Dr. Stephen Covey lists this as the second habit in his book *The 7 Habits of Highly Effective People*.

Having an ending point provides a structured purpose for your plans. No doubt, someone asked you at a very early age what you wanted to be when you grew up. It is a great question to ask yourself repeatedly throughout your life. When asked about their goals upon graduating from a culinary college, students' responses are fascinating. Here is a sampling from a recent incoming freshman class as well as alumni at The Culinary Institute of America:

Ice/fruit carver

Wedding cake designer

Event planner

Ice cream flavor creator

White House chef

Owner of a culinary tourism company

Personal chef to a star (music/TV/film/sports)

Personal shopper

Wine consultant

Forager

Beekeeper

Plate designer

TV personality

Author

Chef at the Vatican

Life coach

Specialty doughnut maker

Food inspector

Research and development chef

Advocate/lobbyist

Clothing designer for foodservice uniforms

Food marketer

Cutlery/tool designer

Coffee roaster

Farmers' market coordinator

Writing Your Goals

Effective goal-setting starts with the process of dreaming big to create the destination, and continues through the process of mapping out the journey. Both aspects of goal-setting are crucial to your success. If we have an end point but no concrete steps to get from here to there, then we may never arrive at our destination. Goals help us to structure our careers and focus our actions in a meaningful way.

Writing goals

Goal-setting is most effective when done with a positive attitude. Start from a place of no limitations by asking yourself this question: What is my dream job? Then, work backward from your dream to create a path that can take you from where you are right now to where you want to be. There are no "can't dos"; this is a process of "can-dos."

This process is based in asking questions — first to determine milestones, and then asking more questions to come up with strategies to reach those milestones.

Setting Up Your Career Filing Cabinet

A "career filing cabinet" is an important part of creating your career and a tactic we refer to throughout this book. You will use it throughout the process of defining and achieving your goals as well as to manage and store the details that go into creating a career. It is a central storage area to hold such important pieces of information as your résumés and cover letters. You will also record and store details of your education and work experiences, details of your professional networks, letters of recommendation, and your professional portfolio. The earlier in your career you create a filing cabinet, and the more often you use it, the more valuable it becomes.

Your career filing cabinet should be an active storage unit, one that you keep organized and updated, ready to use on a regular basis. To get the most out of your cabinet, keep it readily available and easy to access. Make it a habit to visit your cabinet frequently, and keep it organized so that you can manage information and resources as you acquire them, and retrieve them quickly, when you need them.

Using a System

It is easy to become buried by papers, to lose the documents you need during a move, or simply to misplace an important address, phone number, or date. Using a filing system is a good practice for both professional and personal items.

Think about what you are going to be storing and in what form you are likely to have it. Some items may exist only in hard copy. Others may be electronic (which, of course, gives you the option of creating a hard copy). If you prefer to maintain hard-copy records, you will need a place to store materials. The quantity of material you have to file will help you decide whether you need an expanding file folder or a four-drawer filing cabinet, but remember that most experts recommend you double the storage capacity you initially think you need. In addition to a storage container, you will need filing folders, tabs, and labels to identify everything clearly.

Here is an example of this process:

Q: What is my dream job?

A: *To work for the Thomas Keller Restaurant Group (TKRG).*

Q: How do I do that?

A:
1. *Look at TKRG's Web site and check for openings and directions on how to apply.*

2. *Approach people within my network to see if they or their connections have a contact within TKRG.*

3. *Look to work under chefs who have previously worked under Chef Keller, and build a base of experience and a network that will position me to work with Chef Keller later in my career.*

Keep your filing system organized and accessible. Try to avoid letting papers stack up. There is an oft-quoted mantra related to papers: Touch it once. As soon as you have dealt with the requirements of the paper (sent a response, completed an application, and so on), put it in your filing cabinet, in the correct folder.

Keeping materials stored electronically follows the same basic procedure, except that you will not need a physical container, file folders, or tabs. You may need a scanner for items that you do not have as electronic files (for example, school transcripts or letters of recommendation); save them as pdfs or images, and be certain to store the original versions somewhere safe so that you can produce them if required.

Your computer's desktop is an ideal place to create your cabinet. Create a folder, or a shortcut to a folder, which will remain within plain sight on your desktop. This way you can add items easily without the hassle of searching your drive for the folder. Make it a habit to back up your folder to a flash or external hard drive, just in case your computer crashes.

How many folders do you need to organize your career filing cabinet? We suggest starting out with "Goals," "Education," "Experience," "Network Connections," "Mentors," "Résumés," "Cover Letters," "Recommendations," "Achievements," and "Job Prospects." Create more folders and subfolders as you need them.

Cross-Referencing so You Can Find What You Need

Sometimes you may be uncertain about where to file something. Is your internship information filed under Education or Experience? Does the presentation you gave at a workshop at a community center go under Teaching or Volunteering? You do not need to choose, if you take advantage of cross-referencing. Put it where you think it belongs, then make sure that the other folders that might also logically include it have a note or a flag alerting you to where you have actually stored it. This is easy to do, regardless of whether you are filing things electronically (you can use hyperlinks) or manually (add a piece of paper to the file with the specific location).

Each of the points in the last answer can be broken down further to create very specific action steps.

Use the worksheet on page 47 to structure and record your questions and answers. They will become a valuable asset in your career filing cabinet that can help you determine what steps to take on the way to achieving your ultimate goal.

It is important to view goal-setting as an ongoing, fluid process. As you progress in your career, you may find that your interests or circumstances change—what was important ten, five, or even one year ago might no longer be as important. As we evolve, our goals also evolve.

Your goals should provide you with direction and focus, but it is important to remember as you set and review your goals that you need to allow yourself room and permission to stay flexible and adaptable when life does

*M*any people find that they change careers at least once during their working life; others change more often than that. A great number of those entering the foodservice industry are making just such a career change. For some this may be a radical change from the type of work they did in their "previous" life. It is not unusual to find someone who once earned his or her living as an accountant, teacher, or librarian turning to the culinary arts. Victims of downsizing or corporate reorganization have also joined the swelling ranks of those who turn to the culinary world when job leads in one industry or another start to turn cold.

Life experience counts for a great deal. The more you know about yourself before you enter this field, the surer you can be that you will find your way. You may have found yourself constantly fascinated and intrigued with food and cooking, reading cookbooks and magazines voraciously,

and looking for chances to cook new and different dishes for family and friends. You may have found yourself wondering what it would be like to work in a restaurant.

If this describes you, it may be a good idea to take an entry-level position and test the waters. This is a career path quite different from those you might have known before. Advancing through the hierarchy of the kitchen or dining room depends less upon degrees or published papers than on the steady practice of the craft, the application of the technique, and the refinement of the palate.

If you should find that the pressures and hours of working in a kitchen are not suited to your lifestyle or that the adjustments might be too disruptive after years spent at a nine-to-five desk job, do not give up your dream. Look back at the overview in chapter 1; there are many other ways to turn your ambition to work with food into a lucrative and rewarding career.

not go as planned. Goals should be used as a tool for self-awareness, not self-punishment. If circumstances keep you from reaching a goal the way you originally planned, it is time to step back, observe your situation realistically, reassess, evaluate the situation, and begin the process anew.

Types of Goals

There are three main types of goals: short term, intermediate, and long term. In terms of career management, short-term goals are those you plan to accomplish within a year, intermediate goals within five years, and long-term goals in ten years, although these time frames can be adapted and altered to suit your needs. A long-term goal represents your end point, a final destination — your dream job. Achieving these goals requires that you accumulate skills, education, and experience that can only be acquired over time.

With your long-term goals in mind, you can create a timeline that helps identify both immediate (short-term) goals and intermediate goals. Immediate goals are things that you can do right now, or within a relatively short time frame, that will start you on your way. The next goals are the middle steps on the way to your ultimate goal. Your short-term goals will be moving you toward achieving positions that are above your current position and below the final destination. When you consider your options along your career path, you can use your goals to determine whether the step you are planning is helping you get into position to achieve your dream. You can evaluate whether the job responsibilities advance you into a management capacity, for example, or if the opportunity gives you experience with hiring and firing, menu development, or handling budgets. Some positions might have the option of taking college courses as part of your development, which will help you acquire the advanced degree, training, or certification you may need to reach your ultimate goal.

Short-term goals are most immediately attainable, and are also those that meet immediate needs. Short-term goals represent the job you are looking for right now, or the one you currently have, the specific classes you are taking, the books you are reading — they are generally goals you plan to meet over the next six to eighteen months. These are your mise en place, the basic components or building blocks that you will use to reach your intermediate goals — ones that you plan to reach after eighteen months but before three years or so. Just as one element of your mise en place can be used in multiple preparations, short-term goals are the foundations that, when applied correctly, lead to the realization of a number of different intermediate and long-term goals. It is up to you to keep your intermediate and long-term goals in mind as you assess the pros and cons of the jobs you take at the start of your career. A lot of factors come into play.

If you have made thoughtful choices as you take first jobs, you should be able to parlay them into more focused subsequent jobs. You will need to channel the experiences of those first jobs and apply them to the next steps you are planning. **Here is an example of using goals to plan a path from a first job to a dream job:**

Long-Term Goal: Become a Restaurant Manager

Short Term: Short-Term Goals (next two years): Obtain entry-level positions in restaurants. A restaurant manager is responsible for the entire operation, so it is useful to have experience in both kitchens and dining rooms. Seek to work for establishments that have a similar focus and operating style as my long-term goal (concentrating on fine-dining restaurant, or high-volume restaurant, and so forth) to gain greater experience in these types of establishments. Work in the kitchen first (line cook or prep cook), and then move into dining room positions (server).

Intermediate: Intermediate Goals (within three to five years): Transition into positions that offer supervisory opportunities that allow me to build managerial skills. For example, move up from a line cook to a lead line cook or sous chef, or from server to captain. Apply for positions that provide opportunities to demonstrate skills related to hiring and training employees, building teams, and increased responsibility for profitability of business. Start with MIT position as part of a multi-unit chain and advance to assistant manager positions. Make sure to record all of my contributions in my career filing cabinet, including names, positions, and titles of individuals that I report to and that report to me, as well as records of accomplishments and achievements!

Long-Term: Long-Term Goal (within eight to ten years): Achieve position of restaurant manager at the regional or national level for a multi-unit chain. Initiate programs and initiatives that drive business forward using my leadership skills. Mentor those within company that have a drive to be excellent managers themselves.

Making Goals Tangible

Creating goals is a process of reverse engineering, beginning at the end point and working backward until you arrive at your current situation. You need to have a destination in mind to choose the turns you need to make along the way and develop specific plans that move you from your current position to where you want to be.

It is extremely important with goal-setting to write your process down. Use a notebook, sticky pads, spreadsheet, or the planning worksheet below to start researching your dream job.

You need to know not only where you are going, but also what it will take to get you all the way there. Look up real job descriptions and ads from companies or businesses that appeal to you and start making notes. Remember to store them in your career filing cabinet.

Think about the answers to the questions below to get started:

In ten years, I plan to:

1. _____

2. _____

3. _____

4. _____

5. _____

6. _____

7. _____

8. _____

9. _____

10. _____

Within the next five years, I plan to:

1. _____

2. _____

3. _____

4. _____

5. _____

6. _____

7. _____

8. _____

9. _____

10. _____

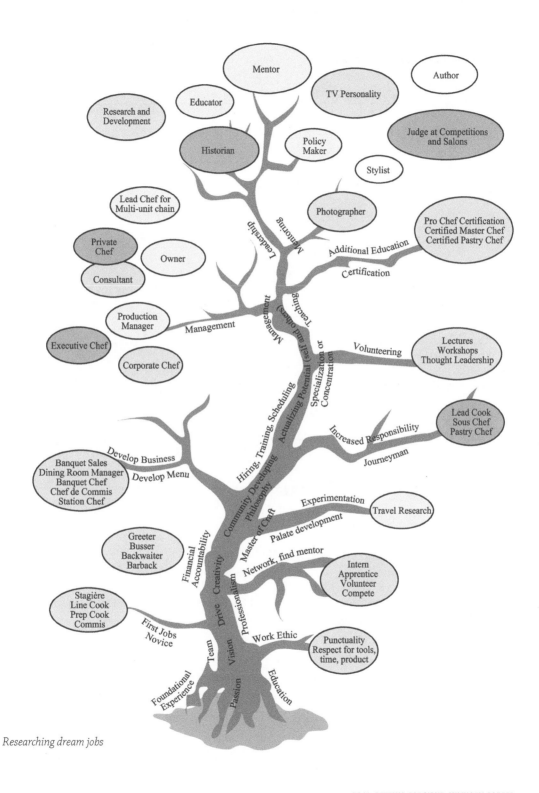

Researching dream jobs

Within the next year, I plan to:

1. _____

2. _____

3. _____

4. _____

5. _____

6. _____

7. _____

8. _____

9. _____

10. _____

Wording Goals

There is research that indicates that the method you use to structure your goals has a direct impact on your ability to achieve them. Dr. Ibrahim Senay conducted research that concluded that those who ask open-ended questions "How may I . . . ?" or "What if I . . . ?" perform better than those who say, "I will . . ." With further inquiry, Senay's research discovered that the severe structuring of goal-setting often shifted the underlying motivational feelings of an individual toward guilt and shame, while the open question inspired a sense of inner responsibility, as described by Clare Plencheck in "The Science of Success with Sam I Am."

Main Folder: Goals

Writing your goals down on paper is the first step in making them tangible. To write goals properly, you will need to do a lot of thinking. If you have done the work properly, it is worth saving.

Store your written goals and any accompanying planning worksheets in your career filing cabinet under the general heading of "Goals." You may want to create subfolders to go more in depth into multiple goals (for instance, Author, Teacher, Executive Chef, and Private Chef) so that you can view, work, and reflect on them consistently.

Subfolders

Create action steps, task lists, and anything else you need that will allow you to chart your progress. These can be filed under headings such as "Short Term" or "Intermediate" as part of the subfolders you have created.

Updating Goals

Sometimes a goal or career direction does not turn out to be what you had expected, and you determine it is best to pursue another avenue. Even if you eventually decide to modify or outright reject a goal, the work that went into creating that goal can be valuable and helpful in achieving other goals toward which you aspire.

Create and store new goals, and keep the record of your achievements with your old goals. You may return to that path at some point, or you may want to share your experiences with others.

Career Goals: Self-Inquiry Exercise

The first step is to dream big. Imagine that you have unlimited possibilities in both your personal life and your professional life. These two facets of your life are intertwined and influence each other. For instance, a dream to live in a certain area can influence your career choices as much as career choices can affect where you live.

Step 1: Generate a list of dream jobs.

Some of us have a clear vision of what we are looking to achieve with our careers and our lives; others are less certain. Ask yourself "What do I like to do?" and "What do I find fulfilling?" and "What brings me joy?" These answers can be anything. Create a list.

If your initial answer to "What (or where) do I want to be in ten years?" was "I don't know," then working through the process of goal-setting can help you clarify some possibilities and evaluate how they match your personal situation. We will continue to use the materials you accumulate throughout this book. You can use the unknowns as a motivation to start a conversation with a mentor or advisor. Keep the answers to "What do I like to do?" and all of the "Whys?" in mind as you read on and during those conversations.

What would you like to do for a career? It is quite possible that you will have many different answers. Write down all of your possibilities.

Step 2: Determine the motivations behind the jobs on your list of possibilities. Asking yourself what appeals to you about a dream job is an important step because it gives you insight into your motivation. Knowing what motivates you gives you insight as to the types of positions and environments where you can be most productive and happiest. The table that follows shows an example of this kind of self-inquiry. Use the blank tables to begin charting your own dreams and motivations.

*H*ow well suited is this industry to accommodating the special concerns of those with families? Workers of both genders are increasingly likely to state that family concerns — day care, time off to care for their families during times of illness, work hours that encourage family time in the evenings and on holidays — are high on their list of priorities.

For those committed to finding or providing family friendly environments, there are solutions to be found. Work hours do vary widely. Bakers and pastry chefs, for instance, often work from the very early hours until just after lunch. Caterers can often control their working hours to establish a schedule that leaves weekdays free for family. Split shifts and shared jobs are all increasingly available, if you are willing to ask.

Others find that the traditional workplace, be it a restaurant, a gourmet shop, or a bakeshop, simply does not have enough flexibility. Instead of trying to shoehorn their "square" lifestyle into a "round" job situation, they are simply breaking out on their own, starting up small businesses and enterprises that help fulfill their culinary aspirations without having to depend upon a system that will not give them enough support to manage their lives and families with comfort.

Ask yourself, "Why do I want to do that?" or "Why do I like that?" Write down the answers. Keep asking "Why?" until you can no longer answer.

Full (Self) Disclosure: Why do I want to do that?

DREAM POSITION	WHAT APPEALS TO ME ABOUT THIS?
Chef-Instructor at a respected culinary school	Prestige; family friendly work hours and days; like working with students/learners; like being in a position of authority; desire to "give back" or "pay it forward"

Creating Intermediate and Short-Term Goals Based on a Long-Term Goal

Once you have a long-term focus (or two, or three, or more), start asking, "What does it take to do this job?" and/or "How does someone get that job?" These questions require some research.

○ **Research the job title.** *You should accumulate a variety of job descriptions that include specific qualifications and job responsibilities.*

○ **Research specific companies or restaurants.** *Try to determine what the overall philosophy is for the company so that you can determine which ones have values and standards that most clearly align with your personal goals.*

○ **Research professional organizations** *for information on specific jobs, certifications, and networking opportunities.*

○ **Identify specific people** *(plug the name of the job into your favorite search engine to find names if you cannot think of any specifics) and research their career paths. Notice their previous positions, education, and length of time they have been doing what they are doing.*

Now you have a tangible description of your dream job as well as an understanding of the education, skills, and qualifications you need to be successful in that position. Ask yourself, "How do I compare with this list right now?" Compare yourself point by point against the required and desired qualifications you found: education, experience, specific skills, and attributes. Look at each point and again ask, "What do I need to do to obtain this skill/qualification/education?" Keep asking "What . . . ?" until you can go no further.

Look at your answers and assign each response an estimated time period for completion. (Hold onto this research, and file it appropriately in your career filing cabinet; for more details about making and maintaining a career filing cabinet, see page 42.) For instance, completing a bachelor's degree takes about four years, while finding an entry-level position typically takes no more than three months. Group the responses into two categories, each based on time of completion: one year or less and between one and five years. These groupings become the foundation for writing your intermediate and short-term goals. Use the worksheet provided on pages 47 and 50 to document your answers.

By following this method, you create an outline for short-term, intermediate, and long-term goals. Only a portion of the work is finished, though. We have traced the steps back from the end to where we are now. Based on this outline, we may now create actual steps to move us from where we are to where we want to be.

Creating intermediate and short-term goals

DREAM POSITION	EXPERIENCE REQUIRED	CURRENT STATUS*	NEXT STEPS	TIME FRAME**
Chef-Instructor at a respected culinary school	Ten years progressively responsible experience	Two years experience with same job title at same company	Can work with current employer and move into higher level positions with more responsiblity. Work for new employer at higher level position	8 years
	At least one management experience desirable	No management	Search for opportunities to train others within current job	3 years
	Certification of CEC (or equivalent) or higher	No certification	Get certification	6 years
	Bachelor's degree or higher	Associate degree	Teach adult ed or continuing ed at local community college. Volunteer to teach cooking classes with organizations (Boy Scouts, Church group, etc.)	anytime

These items should be quantifiable and recorded in your career filing cabinet
**Based on research into required or desired qualification*

Determining intermediate and short-term goals

DREAM POSITION	EXPERIENCE REQUIRED	CURRENT STATUS*	NEXT STEPS	TIME FRAME**

These items should be quantifiable and recorded in your career filing cabinet
** Based on research into required or desired qualification

From Dreams to S.M.A.R.T. Goals

So far, we have defined an end point and have listed a series of possible steps with the potential to move you from where you currently are to that end point. Now we can take these steps and transform them into S.M.A.R.T. goals. The acronym "S.M.A.R.T." contains a very useful method to transform the idea of a goal into a tangible, systematic process to fulfill that goal. This method helps us to create goals that are:

Specific: The goal should be narrow in scope — the more specific you can be, the more effective the rest of the process will be. Look back at the dream job we explored: becoming a chef-instructor at a respected culinary school. If the dream was worded in fairly broad strokes, you need to try to make it more specific. A chef-instructor could teach in a number of different settings. Focusing this dream more narrowly to include an area of specialization (such as breads or Asian cuisine), a type of learning environment (such as a two- or four-year degree-granting institution or a trade school), or even a specific institution will set you up for more effective goal-writing, which will in turn lead to more effective planning.

Measurable: The goal must have a standard to determine when you have succeeded in completing the goal. Again, the more specific the goal, the easier it is to measure. Saying you want to be a famous chef is not an easily measured goal. You want to be famous according to what standard? Saying you want to publish a best-selling cookbook, receive an award or accolade from the International Association of Culinary Professionals or American Culinary Federation, have a television show, or write a blog with several thousand followers is measurable, and any of these might be a way of determining whether or not you are a famous chef. Knowing that you want to be in a particular position within ten years helps you track your progress and make the appropriate adjustments throughout your career. You will not know that you are falling behind if you do not have a timeline to gauge your progress.

Attainable: A goal becomes attainable when specific tasks are created and completed. These tasks are sometimes called "action steps" and are the individual actions that, when completed, result in achievement of the goal. Determining the attainability of a goal is not a yes-or-no question, as all goals are attainable given the right circumstances. Rather it is a question of what: What am I specifically going to do to achieve this goal? A list of action steps gives you a clear list of items to tackle.

These tasks are the foundation work that you will complete on your way to achieving a goal. For example, if your goal is to become a research and development chef, joining the Research Chef's Association and attending a conference are important tasks for you to accomplish. Being clear about how easy or difficult it may be to attain a goal can help you either to rewrite your goal or to take the steps necessary to overcome barriers and obstacles that currently stand in the way, whether financial, personal, or geographic.

Realistic: The goal must be appropriate for you. It should reflect not just a wish, but also how much you are willing and able to do in order to reach your goal. If your goal is to become a food and beverage manager, but your current job is working for a family run business with no chance for advancement, it is not realistic to hold onto that goal unless you are willing and able to make a move into a new work situation where there is room for growth and advancement. What is realistic can and will change based upon where you are in your career and how much progress you have made toward your ultimate goal. It is unrealistic for a novice culinarian to apply for a position as a chef-instructor without enough experience in the culinary arts, even if he or she does have the appropriate teaching experience and college degrees. However, once that same individual accrues the necessary experience, the goal of becoming an instructor becomes very realistic.

Time based: The goal is to be completed within a set amount of time. Timeliness is associated with accountability. Providing a time frame for completion instills a sense of urgency and motivation for completing the goal. Timeliness keeps the goal relevant and provides focus for continued progress.

Organizing a goal, whether it is a short-, intermediate-, or long-term goal, in this way provides focus, a sense of urgency, and accountability. If you are having difficulty with the "specific" and "realistic" aspects, the goal you are attempting to craft may be too large. Continue to ask "What . . . ?" and "How . . . ?" to see if the idea can be further separated into smaller components.

Continuing with this example, we could write the following goal:
"Research at least five culinary schools, and create a chart to compare their programs and cost by the end of the week." Writing this rather broad goal as a S.M.A.R.T. goal starts to show you the specific tasks you will need to undertake to reach it.

Specific:	Complete research and create a chart with points of comparison.
Measurable:	Five different schools are researched and compared.
Attainable:	Use Internet resources (Peterson's, school Web sites, and others); speak with colleagues, friends, mentors, and counselors to see if anyone in my network knows someone who has attended culinary school. Reach out to those people to speak about their experiences.
Realistic:	The amount of work can be accomplished in the given time and with the resources I have available at this point.
Time based:	Complete this by the end of the week.

Completing this goal is a first step on the path to reaching the long-term goal of becoming a chef-instructor.

Making Sense of the Data

One important, and reality-based, aspect of goal-setting for your culinary career is thinking about your salary. You will have expenses to consider, including rent, transportation, food, and clothing at the very least. Most people have loans to repay. Perhaps you have a family to support. Even the passions and hobbies you have outside your career can affect what you need to earn in order to feel like you are making enough to support yourself adequately. While it is a given that entry-level jobs do not pay as much as dream jobs, it is still important to be realistic about where your minimum threshold might fall.

We have assembled some data concerning areas of employment, training, and salaries in Appendix I and Appendix II. This information, although general, can assist in creating your career plan. The positions represented there show the potential for growth in a career, and you can see the progressive increase in responsibility and salary. As responsibilities and salary increase, education and business sense become more important. While people are sometimes promoted into these positions based solely on on-the-job training, the general expectation is that someone in a higher level has more education. If you aspire to a higher level, it may be beneficial to obtain the expected level of education early; the initial investment almost always pays off over time.

You can also use this data for financial planning. If you are entering the culinary world as a novice, it provides a general indication of where you can expect to begin. Early on, it can be useful to limit expenses as much as possible, as the true compensation comes more in the form of experience than wages. As you grow, you become more valuable and can command a higher salary.

Data provides a tangible snapshot of the industry; however, it does not provide guidance on how to approach your culinary career. Each person's career is unique; the first step to creating your career is to begin to establish some goals.

Summary

Creating a long-term career goal is the first step in managing your career. Establishing an end point provides a central structure around which to build your career. With your dream job in mind, you can begin evaluating yourself and researching the position in order to determine what skills, education, and experience you have currently and what you may need to obtain to make your dream a reality. Based on this self-analysis, you can begin to create short-term and intermediate goals — specific steps — that take you from where you are to where you want to be.

Exercises

Exercise 1: Dreaming Big

This exercise is designed to help you explore possibilities and create long-term focal points from which you can create long-term, intermediate, and short-term goals. Answer the questions honestly and without judgment. As Henry Ford said, "Whether you think you can or think you can't, you are correct."

What gives me joy in my life?

_____

_____

_____

What aspects of my current or past jobs or responsibilities did I find the most fulfilling?

_____

_____

_____

What aspects of my current or past jobs or responsibilities did I find the least fulfilling?

_____

_____

_____

What am I good at?

_____

_____

_____

What would I like to be better at?

_____

_____

_____

What motivates and inspires me? Why?

_____

_____

_____

Who motivates and inspires me? Why?

_____

_____

_____

If I could do any type of job, what would it be, and why would I want to do it?

_____

_____

_____

What are the obstacles preventing me from doing that job?

_____

_____

_____

What can I specifically do to overcome those obstacles?

_____

_____

_____

Exercise 2: ## Creating a S.M.A.R.T. Goal

Although the terminology may be different, we create S.M.A.R.T. goals every day, often without realizing it. In order to familiarize yourself with the S.M.A.R.T. methodology, let's apply it to a common event. Transform the following statement into a S.M.A.R.T. goal:

I am going to make dinner tonight.

HINTS:

SPECIFIC: **What am I going to make?**

MEASURABLE: **How will I know that I have completed the task?**

ATTAINABLE: **What specific tasks need to be done to make this meal?**

REALISTIC: **Do I have the materials, time, and skill to make this meal, and can I complete it within the allotted time?**

TIME BASED: **What time will dinner be served tonight?**

three

RÉSUMÉS, COVER LETTERS, AND JOB APPLICATIONS

A RÉSUMÉ IS A PROMOTIONAL TOOL; however, it is also a tool for self-reflection. Since a résumé is a fact-based summary of your experience, education, skills, and accomplishments, writing a résumé gives you the opportunity to observe yourself objectively and compare your qualifications directly with the desired qualifications of the job you are seeking.

There is not one perfect way to create a résumé. Every writer and reader is different. Every position is different. As you progress in your career, keep your résumé current. This living, fluid document can, should, and will change over time. Even though there are limitless possibilities when creating a résumé, remember that it is *about* you, but it is *for* the potential employer.

A cover letter, which typically accompanies your résumé, is a different way to present yourself. Instead of listing facts and details about your education and experience, it allows you to put those details into context and make them relevant to your employer. Both your résumé and your cover letter are vital components in any serious job application process. The job application itself may call for these two documents, and the process of applying for a job can be a clear indication of how well you will "fit" with your potential employer.

Résumés

Think of your résumé as an amuse-bouche: a single perfect bite that encompasses the totality of your skills and leaves the guest wanting more. The experience created by the résumé is a demonstration of how you work. Is it well structured, balanced, easy to read, and error-free? These are positive things. Is it imbalanced, difficult to read (hard-to-read font, point size too large or too small), and riddled with errors (spelling, inconsistent punctuation, verb tense agreement, or inaccuracies in degree or job title listings)? This demonstrates to a potential employer the effort (or lack thereof) you will put into the job if hired.

Your résumé is generally the first point of contact with a potential employer. It is an introduction, something to spark interest; in short, it is a commercial. Think for a minute about commercials you have seen. During a half-hour TV show, approximately eight minutes of time is devoted to commercial advertisements. Most of these commercials run for about thirty seconds. This is not a long time. During this half hour, you are a captive audience, meaning that you most likely will watch the entire show. However, during the commercial breaks, advertisers are competing with your need to use the restroom, get a snack, talk to your friends and family, and so on. They need to get their message to you quickly and memorably. Advertisers target specific audiences. Compare the commercials during a children's show, an hour-long drama, and a sports game. Notice that sometimes the volume of commercials is louder than the show, so you can still hear it if you leave the room. Notice the use of catchy music or phrases that the advertisers hope will stay stuck in your head. Not a single item is accidental. Every sound, image, and color in that commercial is designed to sell that product. Your résumé should function in the same way — it must get its message across quickly and leave a lasting impression on the reader. Your résumé will contain the details of your work experience and your education, although the type of résumé style you choose will determine exactly which components you include and how you position them on the finished document. We begin by looking at the basic elements of a typical résumé.

Résumé FAQs

Q How long should a résumé be?

A: *Your résumé should be as long as it needs to be to sell you to the prospective employer effectively. That being said, there are some rules to keep in mind. First, create your résumé with the understanding that it will get about fifteen seconds of attention. Let someone read your résumé when you think it's ready. Time that person for fifteen seconds, then ask him or her to summarize your experiences in broad terms. If that person cannot, that is a good indication that the document is too long or that the information is too dense. Generally, one page is sufficient, unless you have extensive experience. If you do go onto a second page, it should be a complete page. Remember to include your heading (contact information) on the second page as well.*

Q Do I need to include "References Available on Request?"

A: *This is unnecessary. If you are applying for a job, it is understood that you will provide references if asked.*

Q Can I put a list of references on my résumé?

A: *A list of references is a separate document (see Letters of Recommendation, page 84). Your résumé is a taste, an introduction; it generates interest. If you give a potential employer all of your information at one time, there is no reason for anyone to speak with you to find out more information.*

Q Do I really need a résumé? Can I get a job without one?

A: *A résumé is an advertisement, another way of communicating. It is not always possible to meet initially with an employer face-to-face or on the phone. Neither is it always possible to receive a direct recommendation for a position. A résumé is an asset in these situations. Employers tend to get more applicants than they have openings. If a candidate looks good but does not fit the immediate need, an employer may keep his or her résumé on file. Most employers expect that any true professional will have a résumé. A well-crafted document demonstrates pride in your career path, the ability to communicate effectively, and the idea that you care enough about the potential employer to provide an accurate account of your professional history.*

Contact Information

The first, and arguably the most important, section of any résumé is contact information. Any other information, as well as content, formatting, and paper selection, is wasted if a potential employer cannot find your name and contact information easily. Your name and contact information should act as the anchor of the résumé, the first and last thing a potential employer reads. It should be self-contained, meaning that in one glance the employer will see both your name and immediate contact information.

Common Résumé Traps to Avoid

1. Using "I." If you read the sample résumés, you can see that the word "I" is unnecessary; your reader is already assuming that the subject is "I."

2. Starting bullets with the same word. Even if what follows the first word is not repetitive, the overall effect is that of repetition. If the reader is skimming, he or she will not see past the repeated word.

3. Spelling errors. If you are going to use the French brigade titles, please make sure to use them accurately and spell them properly. For a list of traditional station titles, see the table on pages 6–8.

Résumé Formats and Templates

The type of résumé you write will determine which pieces of information you provide and in what order you present them. The header for your résumé is an important element. Here are some different header styles you can consider.

The first example is centered, much like how we are used to seeing a title or chapter heading in a book. It is balanced in the center of the page, with even amounts of negative (white) space to either side. The mailing address, e-mail address, and phone number are framed below the name.

John Smith

EMAIL aaabbb@email.com
555 West Fifth Street • Hometown, AL 55555
HOME (123) 456-7890 CELL (555) 555-555

Résumé header example 1

The second example is justified left. We habitually look at the top left corner of the page first; this arrangement capitalizes upon that habit. Here, the e-mail is listed first, followed by phone number and mailing address. In an electronic world, e-mail is the easiest and quickest way to respond, so this method of contact is given primary placement, on the left margin just below or just above the name.

EMAIL aaabbb@email.com
HOME (123) 456-7890 CELL (555) 555-555
555 West Fifth Street • Hometown, AL 55555

John Smith

Résumé header example 2

555 West Fifth Street
Hometown, AL 55555

HOME (123) 456-7890
CELL (555) 555-555
EMAIL aaabbb@email.com

John Smith

Résumé header example 3

Although a common layout option, the third example may not be as effective as the others. Since we read top down, left to right, the first place the eye naturally falls (top left) is blank, negative space in this example. The reader has to scan over to the right. The eye may land on the contact information first, because it is closest to the center of the page. If this happens, the reader may naturally want to follow the line, and then move to the next one down. To see the name, the reader has to break normal flow and look up the page. If the eye goes first to the bold name, the natural flow is to continue to skim down the page. Again, the reader's normal tendency is disrupted; now he or she needs to return to the left side of the page to continue reading.

Why is this important? In the first two examples, the writer has played into the reader's natural tendencies, giving vital information where it is most easily seen. In the third, the reader has to disrupt natural tendency. This slight feeling of disruption may create a certain negative feeling for the reader ("This is hard to read!") for the entire document. With only about fifteen seconds, the job seeker does not have a lot of time to turn around negative feelings.

Education

"Education" on a résumé refers to formal degree- or certificate-bearing programs of study.

Since your résumé is an accurate account of your history, all information must be correct. This document becomes part of your application, and any

Education

Formal Education

An accurate record of your education, degrees, certifications, and professional training is vital when applying for jobs. Much of the value to be gained from these credentials depends upon the conferring institution and date received. As you accumulate degrees and certifications and attend training sessions, it may become difficult to remember the exact relevant titles, dates, and certifying bodies. Having a running list allows you to keep this information accurate and up to date.

Many employers complete background checks as a matter of course, and inconsistencies between your application and other records may take you out of consideration. This could be something as simple as listing a degree incorrectly (listing AAS when you received an AOS, for example). To be certain that you do not inadvertently misrepresent your education, keep accurate records in your career filing cabinet.

Professional Development

In addition to formal degree programs, you may build your professional knowledge through classes, workshops, and certifications. Often, you will receive a certificate documenting your attendance or level of mastery. As with formal education, it is vital to accurately represent your professional development. Remember to keep your certificates and any course materials in your filing cabinet!

Informal Education

It is important for professionals to stay current in their field and to continue to build their expertise through self-directed research, reading, study, and experimentation. In some cases, experience gained by means of community service, teaching a workshop, or giving a lecture may be appropriate to list on your résumé. In others, it will become part of your portfolio (see page 421). Even if you are not able to list your informal education on a résumé, the knowledge gained will contribute to your career's success. Record the details of your self-guided education: books you have read, community events at which you have volunteered, recipes you have developed, and so forth.

Checklist for Education Files

- ☐ Name of School
- ☐ Address
- ☐ Years of attendance
- ☐ Degree received
- ☐ Area of study
- ☐ Unofficial transcript (with GPA and class rank)
- ☐ Awards and recognitions
- ☐ Clubs and organizations
- ☐ Contact information (phone numbers or Web Site to acquire official transcripts, for example)

Checklist for Professional Development or Continuing Education Files

- ☐ Name of course/workshop/certification
- ☐ Institution or certifying body
- ☐ Date awarded
- ☐ Date of expiration
- ☐ Number of CEU (continuing education credits)
- ☐ Name of instructor

discrepancies between your résumé, formal application (if required), and background check (if performed) can immediately remove you from consideration or, if employed, may be cause for immediate termination.

Be sure to include the name and full address (street, city, state, and country) of the institution (or certificate-issuing entity), the name of the degree or certificate being pursued, and the year in which it was (or will be) conferred. Under most circumstances, it is not customary or expected that you include any specific information about the degree, such as a list of courses.

List the most recent experience first; alternatively, you may want to list the highest degree first, if the most recent experience is not the highest level of education you possess. It is acceptable to list programs in which you are currently enrolled and programs that you did not complete.

High school may be listed; however, it generally comes off the résumé after you have attained a higher degree, or if it has been more than five years since graduation.

See examples of how to list education in the accompanying sample résumés:

Single degree from one institution:

The Culinary Institute of America Hyde Park, NY, April 2010
    Associate in Occupational Studies, Culinary Arts

Multiple degrees from one institution:

The Culinary Institute of America Hyde Park, NY
    Bachelor of Professional Studies, Baking and Pastry Arts Management,
    April 2010
Associate in Occupational Studies, Baking and Pastry Arts,
    January 2009

Degree in progress:

The Culinary Institute of America Hyde Park, NY
    Candidate for Associate in Occupational Studies, Culinary Arts
    Anticipated Graduation April 2012

Multiple degrees from multiple institutions:

State University of New York at New Paltz, NY, May 2007

Master of Business Administration

Marist College, Poughkeepsie, NY, May 2005

Bachelor of Science, International Studies

The Culinary Institute of America Hyde Park, NY, April 2010

Associate in Occupational Studies, Culinary Arts

ISLAND RESORT, ISLAND, FL

SOUS CHEF   **2008 – PRESENT**

Direct a staff of up to seven crew members in kitchen operations. Oversee menu development and implementation. Maintain food cost and inventory controls. Expedite lunch and dinner services. Provide employee training. Perform light office duties – including staff scheduling and payroll. Organize banquet production, and oversee proper execution of banquet meals.

Sample résumé entry: modified paragraph

ISLAND RESORT, ISLAND, FL

SOUS CHEF   **2008 – PRESENT**

- Direct a staff of up to seven crew members in kitchen operations.

- Oversee menu development and implementation.

- Maintain food cost and inventory controls.

- Expedite lunch and dinner services.

- Provide employee training.

- Perform light office duties – including staff scheduling and payroll.

- Organize banquet production, and oversee proper execution of banquet meals.

Sample résumé entry: bulleted

*A*ction verbs carry meaning. Using action verbs in a résumé and cover letter will assertively present your qualifications and highlight your achievements.

Technical Skills

Baked
Blended
Braised
Broiled
Butchered
Cleaned
Cooked
Cured
Decorated
Fabricated
Filled
Finished
Folded
Fried
Garnished
Glazed
Grilled
Hosted
Iced
Laminated
Mixed
Molded
Ordered
Piped
Plated
Poached
Portioned
Purchased
Received
Rotated
Roasted
Rolled
Sautéed
Scaled
Served
Shaped
Sliced
Smoked
Specialized
Steamed
Stored
Tasted
Washed

Achievements

Accomplished
Achieved
Acquired
Applied
Delivered
Demonstrated
Doubled
Earned
Enhanced
Exceeded
Expanded
Fulfilled
Halved
Helped
Improved
Increased
Presented
Received
Reduced
Reinforced
Restored
Strengthened
Succeeded
Surpassed
Transformed
Tripled
Won

Interpersonal Skills

Adapted
Advised
Analyzed
Assessed
Assisted
Clarified
Controlled
Corrected
Mediated

Design/Presentation Skills

Assembled
Built
Completed
Composed
Conceived
Constructed
Controlled
Created
Decreased
Designed
Developed
Enhanced
Established
Expanded
Formed
Formulated
Founded
Improved
Increased
Invented
Operated
Prepared
Presented
Produced
Reduced
Researched
Set up
Standardized
Started
Utilized
Worked

Managerial Skills

Acted
Administered
Assigned
Consulted
Delegated
Directed
Employed
Guided
Handled
Hired
Interviewed
Managed
Organized
Oversaw
Represented
Scheduled
Staffed
Supervised
Trained

Planning Skills

Anticipated
Arranged
Budgeted
Calculated
Collaborated
Communicated
Conducted
Coordinated
Distributed
Evaluated
Expedited
Identified
Maintained
Organized
Priced
Programmed
Projected

Main Folder: Experience

During the course of your career, you may hold several "steady" jobs that you will list on your résumé. You may also have numerous opportunities to acquire experience that is different from that gained at a typical job. For instance, you may volunteer at events (related to your field or not), participate in conferences, or perform one-time jobs (like catering an event). Each of these experiences may become a valuable promotional tool for you in the future. You may be able to list some of these experiences on your résumé, you may mention them in a cover letter, or you may talk about them in an interview.

Most immediately, potential employers want to know where you have worked (usually no further than ten years in the past, but for some positions, like government jobs, it is customary to supply a detailed, exhaustive work history). Businesses may close, be sold, or be renamed and your employment records can be lost, unless you keep them in your career filing cabinet.

Create a list of every work experience (paid or volunteer, steady or per diem), with the name of the employer, name of the supervisor (if applicable), address, phone number, dates of employment or volunteering, and Web address (if applicable), and follow each entry with a brief description of what you did and the contributions you made. Be sure to include your rate of pay as well. The details

of your salary history may be important both during the application process (for instance, if you are asked to supply either a salary history or salary requirements) and during negotiations following a job offer.

Just as there are "formal" and "informal" subfolders for education, your work history can include these subfolders:

- Volunteering.

- Community service.

- Expert on a subject as verified by interviews, media appearances, consulting (although you should list paid consulting work as part of your formal work experiences).

- Writing in the form of articles, books, curriculum, blogs, reviews, or critiques.

Experience

The experience section is the real selling point of the résumé. This section provides the proof that you have the skills and abilities to do the job. An employer can look at this section and see if you have occupied a similar role in the past, your progression, and your length of time at each position, and the employer can begin to assess the quality of your experience.

Basic expected information in this section includes the name and location (city/state) of the employer, dates of employment (m/y–m/y), title, and (in most cases) a description of your responsibilities.

As with education, it is vital that the names, locations, and dates of employment be accurate. The exact mailing address, phone, URL, and name of supervisor are not needed — remember that this is an advertisement for you, not for a past employer. If you have held several titles during your term of employment, list the employer once. You may elect to list and describe the positions held as subentries, to demonstrate progressively responsible experience. Or in the interest of space, you may elect to list only your last title and mention your progression within the description itself.

Under each experience, create a list of accomplishments and duties that you performed at that job. This can be done either in a modified paragraph format or as a bulleted list.

Regardless of the format, these descriptions need not be written in complete sentences. The reader knows that the subject is "I." Lead with action verbs, and vary the verbs used to keep the reader from becoming bored. Focus on accomplishments as opposed to job duties. Accomplishments make you unique and demonstrate your initiative, whereas job duties are merely the tasks that were assigned to you.

Additional Elements on a Résumé

"Education" and "Experience" are the two main sections of your résumé. There are several more ancillary sections that may be useful at times. These include an objective, awards that you have received, certifications, and organizations to which you belong.

Objective

An objective may be useful if you are applying for a specific position and are not including an introductory letter, although it is not essential on all résumés. An objective is just that: the immediate purpose of the résumé submission. It is not a statement of your career goals, your personal philosophy, or a biographical summation. Give some thought to this short statement. Use an objective to speak about what you can offer rather than what you can gain from the experience.

Do you have to include an objective? Not always. Space on your résumé is valuable. If your introductory letter or e-mail already includes the details of the position for which you are applying, you might be better off without an objective. You will have more space to highlight your educational background and work experiences.

If you do include an objective, keep it brief. Avoid buzzwords or giving the impression that you are selfish. **Objectives are most effective when they are specific to the position you are looking for and speak to what you can offer:**

"To obtain a position as a line cook with the Marriott Marquis."

"To provide an exceptional dining experience to the guests of Restaurant Daniel."

Certifications, Activities, Awards, Professional Organizations

These sections may be listed under separate headings or combined under one heading, depending upon how much information you would like to present. Your entries should be both relevant and current; for example, high-school activities are no longer current once you have completed college. They should be specific as well; "running" is not as appropriate as "member of Mid Hudson Runner's Club." Group like items together, and be consistent with your format.

A word of caution: Since employers are forbidden from discriminating based on sex, race, religion, and national origin, it is usually prudent to omit any affiliations you may have with associations that might be particularly polarizing, such as political or religious groups, especially if they are not relevant to your ability to perform the job you seek.

When creating a résumé, you can either design the document yourself or use a template. Crafting a résumé from scratch is a skill every job seeker should possess. A template is useful if you desire a bit of graphic style but do not possess the skills to create it yourself, but keep in mind that you may have difficulty adjusting the template if your information does not exactly match.

Your résumé must be clear, concise, and easy to read. The template (if you are using one), fonts, colors, and paper should all enhance your résumé to this end. If you are feeling unsure as to whether a template, font, color, or type of paper works, have a mentor or friend review it.

Choosing a Template, Fonts, Colors, and Paper

Selecting a Structure for Your Résumé

The actual layout, style, and exact information you will provide in a final draft will depend greatly upon the position for which you are applying and the company to which you are applying. Companies often produce different commercials for the same product in order to appeal to a specific target audience. The ad you see for the exact same make and model of car might be quite different on a major network like CBS than it would be on a special-interest channel like ESPN. Likewise, you may want to prepare different versions of your résumé to target different potential employers.

First, consider your audience. Keep in mind that the person reading your résumé is busy, so he or she will probably just skim the document to decide whether it is worth a closer read. Ten, fifteen, twenty seconds is all that you have to entice that reader to give your résumé a second, more thorough, look. In Western cultures, we read from top to bottom and left to right; if you arrange your information in that layout, it is easier for the reader. The eye is attracted to contrast and notices the contrast before the content. We also expect symmetry (balance), and any disruption to a sym-

When submitting your résumé electronically, it is best to follow the employer's directions as to how this should be done. You may be directed to paste it into the body of an e-mail or to upload the file if you are applying online.

If there is no specific direction, it is common to send an e-mail with the résumé as an attachment. You should take the extra step of converting your résumé to either a pdf file or an image file to preserve the formatting and styling choices you have made to ensure that the potential employer views it as you intend it to be seen.

After creating your résumé in the word-processing program of your choice, convert it to a pdf file. Some word-processing programs have this option built in. If not, a free converter may be downloaded at the CutePDF Web site. Alternatively, you could convert or scan your résumé into a picture format (.jpg or .gif). It is always best to indicate the format of your attachment in the body of the e-mail: "I have attached my résumé, in pdf format . . ."

metrical layout draws our attention. With this in mind, we can position the most important and relevant information at the top and along the left margin, and then use combinations of boldface, point size, and font to create visual interest and to attract the eye to the information we want the reader to see.

Once you have selected the appropriate items from your inventory of work experiences and education, it is time to put it all together.

First, consider both the potential employer and the job for which you are applying. A posted opening often includes a list of specific skills and qualifications the employer is seeking, along with a description of the job itself. If the advertisement does not supply this information, search for advertisements for similarly titled positions. The details may not be the same in every company, but you will still have a better understanding of what the job title means, the duties that go along with it, and the attributes you will need to succeed.

Look to your career filing cabinet. Are there elements within your past positions that match closely to this new position? Are there qualifications that are not requested but that will set you apart from other candidates? Are there accomplishments and activities that you are proud of but that have no bearing on this job or employer? Leave these latter items out. Recall that this document is about you but created for them. It needs to demonstrate that you are what they want.

Having decided upon specific content, layout is next. There are four basic résumé formats.

Chronological

Chronological résumés are the most common and the most versatile. The entries within the "Education" and "Experience" sections are listed in reverse chronological order (most recent first, then moving back in time). Descriptions follow each entry.

Education is listed before experience if you are still in school or have recently graduated. Once you gain some experience, that category takes the lead. As you put the information to the page, recall again that we read top to bottom, left to right, and that the eye sees contrast and changes in symmetry before processing the words.

Jamie Applicant

1234 NW 99th Avenue • Anytown, FL 12345
(987) 654-3210 • chef@email.com

BACKGROUND:

Well-educated, trained, and experienced Executive Chef with more than 18-years of exemplary service in the culinary field. Proven success at restaurants ranging from casual to upscale high-end cuisine. Expertise in a myriad of culinary styles including: American, European, Russian, Italian, French, Caribbean, Asian, exotic game, steak, seafood, pastry, and desserts. Significant restaurant and employee management experience, coupled with an ability to deliver superior guest satisfaction, while maintaining profitability requirements. Skilled at developing creative, distinctive, and profitable menus. A trusted resource that brings energy, dedication, and a respected approach to the profession.

EXPERIENCE:

DS Hotel, Miami Lakes, FL   **2008 – Present**

Consists of two hotels, the DS Hotel and The Blue Hotel at the Golf Club, totaling 280 rooms. Collective revenue: $35M.

Chronological résumé

Functional

A *functional résumé* takes a slightly different approach. The experience section is a list: employer, location, title, and dates, with no description. This style uses additional sections ("Summary of Qualifications" and/or "Highlights of Experiences".) Accomplishments, skills, and attributes are listed in these sections rather than with each job. A functional style is useful for someone with exten-

Jamie Applicant

1234 NW 99th Avenue • Anytown, FL 12345
(987) 654-3210 • chef@email.com

BACKGROUND:

Well-educated, trained, and experienced Executive Chef with more than 18-years of exemplary service in the culinary field. Proven success at restaurants ranging from casual to upscale high-end cuisine. Expertise in a myriad of culinary styles including: American, European, Russian, Italian, French, Caribbean, Asian, exotic game, steak, seafood, pastry, and desserts. Significant restaurant and employee management experience, coupled with an ability to deliver superior guest satisfaction while maintaining profitability requirements. Skilled at developing creative, distinctive, and profitable menus. A trusted resource that brings energy, dedication, and a respected approach to the profession.

SELECTED ACHIEVEMENTS:

- Built and managed successful teams of 36+ employees.

- Direct P&L responsibility working with the Food and Beverage Director to achieve budgetary goals.

Functional résumé

sive experience, allowing them to present maximum information in a minimum of space. This style can also be useful for career changers with no direct, titled experience in the industry they are seeking. Listing transferable skills, those skills that apply across many industries, first focuses the reader on the applicant's skills, rather than on the applicant's employment history.

Hybrid

The third category of résumé is a *hybrid* of the chronological and functional styles. A purely functional résumé demands that the employer spend some time reading it; they can be wordier than a chronological résumé. The advantages of both a functional and a chronological résumé are present in a hybrid résumé. The document is essentially divided into two parts: qualifications and job narrative. The "Qualifications" section of this résumé is usually shorter than the functional portion of a functional résumé, but it still introduces the

PO Box 123 | 987.654.3210
Anytown, FL | EMAIL aaabbb@email.com

ANDREW JOBSEEKER

SOUS CHEF / CHEF DE CUISINE / KITCHEN MANAGER

Excellent Culinary Skills • Skilled Inventory Management • Staff Training

Motivated, highly skilled Sous Chef with an extensive track record of skillfully training and leading culinary staff, proficiently directing kitchen processes and operations in an efficient manner, and deftly creating menus with an utmost attention to quality ingredients, exceptional presentation, and creativity.

SELECTED CAREER HIGHLIGHTS

- Maintained Food Cost Percentage of 27% or lower while maintaining high food-quality standards.

- Directed processes toward achieving a Labor Cost Percentage of 18% or lower through maintaining proper scheduling and business forecasting.

Hybrid résumé

candidate's core strengths. The "Job Narrative" section provides the context for the qualifications you claim to have.

Curriculum Vitae (CV)

A fourth type of résumé, known as a *curriculum vitae (CV)*, may have limited use when you are applying for jobs, since it typically includes more personal information than employers in the United States want to see, including pieces of

CINDY APPLICANT

CHEF

PERSONAL INFORMATION

- Date of Birth: 16 June 1985
- US Citizen
- Marital Status: Single, no children
- Non smoking/No visible tattoos

OBJECTIVE

To find employment as either a private or charter Chef with opportunity to travel.

EXPERIENCE

Chef. 90' Ferretti, *M/Y Nutmeg*. November 2009 – April 2010

Curriculum vitae

Letters of recommendation offer a "second opinion" for any claims that you have made about yourself. These letters come from trusted sources: current or former employers or supervisors, instructors, coaches, and clients. The strongest recommendations come from those who have directly observed your work. They offer specific, objective (not based upon opinion) accounts of times when you have demonstrated value.

Obtaining Letters of Recommendation

Oftentimes a potential employer will ask for a list of references as a part of the application process, and it is expected that you will provide them when asked. You do not have to wait until you are in the job search process to ask someone for a recommendation! It is actually more beneficial to ask for a recommendation while your good work is fresh in their minds, as opposed to asking them to remember later.

The easiest way to obtain a general letter of recommendation (one that speaks to your good work and abilities) is to ask for it. Offer some direction to the writer: "I am building my portfolio and was wondering if you would be willing to write a letter of recommendation for me? When I started, I could barely hold a knife, and now I am running my own station on the busiest nights. I am grateful for the opportunity and training you have given me." Add this letter to your portfolio. Now you can provide a copy (not the original) to a potential employer immediately upon request.

During the job search, a letter that mentions the specific characteristics or skill sets you possess makes it easier for a potential employer to evaluate how well you fit the needs of a particular position. Ask the appropriate connection to write a letter that highlights these traits (you will know what they are if you have done your research properly).

You might write or say something along these lines: "I am applying to [company name] for a management position. I know I can do this job well, but I do not have titled management experience on my résumé. Could you please write me a letter of recommendation that highlights my leadership abilities? When I worked for you, I trained several new hires. . . ."

Points to Remember

- A mediocre or general letter of recommendation is worse than no letter. Have a conversation with the writer so that he or she knows about specific items to highlight.

- The impact of a recommendation comes from the fact that it was provided by a trusted source. Proofread all letters that are given to you. An error-filled letter diminishes the credibility of the source.

- It is not appropriate for family members or friends to offer recommendations. These letters should come from positions of authority and speak specifically about your abilities as they relate to your profession.

- Letters should be signed by the writer. If you are requesting a letter directed toward a specific opportunity, have the writer address the employer directly.

- Keep all originals in your filing cabinet. They can be scanned or copied. Assume that anything you hand across the desk or send in the mail to a potential employer will not be returned to you.

information that will spell out age, ethnicity, religion, or other factors. While a résumé is brief and concise — no more than a page or two — a CV is longer and more detailed. It includes a summary of your educational and academic backgrounds, teaching and research experience, publications, presentations, awards, honors, affiliations, and other details. In Europe, the Middle East, Africa, and Asia, employers may expect to receive a curriculum vitae. In the United States, a CV is appropriate when applying for academic, education, scientific, or research positions, as well as fellowships or grants.

Cover Letter

Your résumé is your fact sheet — it is a marketing tool with factual, objective information that supports your claim that you are the best candidate for the position. No matter how you format it, your résumé is a list of facts. It is a well-presented and focused list certainly, but a list nonetheless. The complement to this list is a cover letter. The cover letter serves as an introduction. It gives the reader a reason to look at your résumé. It creates a connection between writer and reader, and it serves to direct the reader's attention to your strongest qualifications. If the résumé is a fifteen- to thirty-second commercial, the cover letter is your five-second pitch.

The term *cover letter* came about because at one time, résumés and letters were invariably supplied as hard copy. An introductory letter lay on top of the résumé, covering it. When the reader opened the envelope, the letter of introduction was the first item the recipient read. Today, this piece of communication may still be a physical letter on a piece of paper, but it may also be an e-mail to which you have attached your résumé. Unlike the résumé, it is important to address format first, before content.

The style of writing of a cover letter is a bit different from how we are used to communicating. Many of us feel uncomfortable when we present our accomplishments. We may feel like we are bragging or trying to sell something. When you are writing a cover letter, you *are* bragging and trying to sell something (you). That is the explicit purpose. You are highlighting your qualities, yet this is not a page of "I am awesome!" Rather, it is a purposefully measured combination of expressing your features (what makes you unique) and explaining how you will benefit that employer.

Traditional Cover Letter

The letter itself has three main content sections followed by a conclusion. By answering the following questions, the letter will begin to write itself: Why am I writing this letter (what is the purpose or expected outcome)? Why do I want to work for this particular employer? What do I have to offer this particular employer (in other words, why should they hire me)?

A cover letter, and any professional correspondence, is part of your formal application for a job, so the tone, wording, and presentation should demonstrate that you are a professional. When sending a printed letter, it should be set in business letter format, typed single-spaced, signed in blue (highly recommended) or black ink, and one page in length.

The Hook

We have already stated that a cover letter is more conversational and personal than a résumé, and it is only one page in length. Even though conversational, you still need to be brief and to the point. Opening your letter with your purpose engages and focuses the reader immediately. The reader understands what you are looking for and can begin to adjust his or her thinking. If you are applying for an advertised position, a specific type of cover letter called an *application letter* should be used. The opening may look like this: "I am writing to apply for the position of Editorial Assistant, which was advertised on Starchefs' Web site."

The Pitch

Having focused the reader's attention, the next step is to create interest. One of Stephen Covey's habits in *The 7 Habits of Highly Effective People* is "Seek first to understand, then be understood." By listening, understanding, and empathizing, you can accomplish more than you can through talking, asserting, and overpowering. We can use a similar mindset when writing cover letters. After communicating your focus or intent, think about answering the question, Why do I want to work for this employer? With this question, you are seeking to make a connection, to demonstrate that you have an understanding of the employer's business, their place in the industry, their successes, and their challenges. You are creating a relationship between writer and reader, a human-

Checklist for Cover Letters

☐ **The letter** needs to be addressed and sent to an individual. "To Whom It May Concern" does not concern anyone. Use the Internet or call the location and ask to whom you should send your application.

☐ **The salutation** should be formal: Dear Mr./Ms. (or title, if appropriate) Last name:

☐ **Proofread** for spelling, grammar, punctuation, and capitalization. This is not a text message, and a potential employer is not your friend. Capitalizing their name and establishment and addressing them as a professional (Ms. Smith, Chef Smith, Dr. Smith) is a sign of respect. Capitalizing "I" demonstrates that you have respect for yourself.

☐ **Each letter** should be customized to a specific employer. There are times when similar letters may be sent to multiple employers. If you do create a template, be certain all names used are correct to the employer you are addressing. Sending an application to the Hyatt but mentioning your desire to work at the Marriot ensures prompt deletion.

☐ **If sending** a hard copy, sign your name in blue ink. It stands out from the black ink of the text, and adds a personal touch.

☐ **Formal tone** does not mean pseudo-legal or pseudo-business speak. The voice of the letter should be your voice, albeit more polished and professional than your conversational voice. This tone should be consistent through all contact, including the initial letter, follow up e-mails, phone conversations, and in person interviews.

Checklist for cover letters

to-human connection. If you were referred to this contact by another person, mention this person right away to establish the connection.

Now you are ready to give your pitch by answering the question, Why should you hire me? When answering this question, think in terms of specific skills, accomplishments, and experience that you have that can directly benefit the individual employer. These specifics should reference, but not repeat, information on your résumé. The cover letter calls attention

123 MAIN STREET
HOMETOWN, FL 12345
NOVEMBER 1, 2012

Mr. John Smith
DIRECTOR OF HUMAN RELATIONS
5 Star Hotel
25 Street Ave.
Anywhere, CA 56789

Dear Mr. Smith:

Please consider me for the Assistant Front of the House Manager position that was advertised this week with The Culinary Institute of America's Career Services Office. My enthusiasm and discipline combined with my work experience and education from The Culinary Institute of America make me an excellent candidate for this position.

As indicated in my résumé, I am graduating with a Bachelor's Degree in Culinary Arts Management in January of 2006. This academic program combined with my previous experience has allowed me to develop my managerial skills. On Externship at the Four Seasons, Atlanta, I learned the dedication and commitment to excellence that it takes to meet the expectatons of discriminating customers who anticipate the best. My years of working as a server in various restaurants have developed my customer service and interpersonal skills and have fostered my passion for the hospitality industry.

Once you have reviewed my enclosed résumé, I would welcome the opportunity to speak with you about my qualifications in further detail and to learn more about this position. I can be reached on my cell at 845/123-4567 or by e-mail at jake-hudson@isp.com. Thank you for your time and consideration, and I look forward to speaking with you.

Sincerely,

Jake Hudson

Jake Hudson

Sample cover letter: standard business format

to specifics and guides the reader to draw conclusions about these specifics, and the résumé provides the factual details to validate the claims you are making.

If you are applying to an advertised position, be sure to give examples to match the list of qualifications. If the advertisement states "Fine-dining establishment seeks experienced manager," then you know you must demonstrate that you have both fine-dining experience and managerial experience. If you do not have these two qualifications, highlight similar skill sets. In this example, managerial skill sets would include hiring, training, coaching, guest interaction, conflict resolution, and financial accountability, among others.

The Clincher

Cover letters finish with a formal conclusion. Thank the reader for his or her time, and set the expectation for another point of contact: "Thank you for considering my application. I look forward to your prompt response. I can be reached by phone at (123) 455-7890 or e-mail at ronaldjobseeker@email.com." Here you have professionally asserted the expectation of a response, and you have made it easy for the employer to respond by providing your contact information.

Envelope

With a written letter, the true first impression the recipient has is of the envelope. The address on the envelope should be typed or very neatly handwritten, and the recipient's name and title and the company's name must be correct and accurate. Take care as well when positioning the stamp. The recipient may not notice these little details when done well; however, if the envelope is sloppy or the recipient's name, title, or company is incorrect, it will color his or her initial perception of you. A guest will most likely never make any mention of a clean glass, but a glass with spots will surely gain negative attention.

E-Mail

For an e-mail, the format differs slightly from that of a hard-copy printed letter. Your e-mail carrier already provides the addresses and dates. Since it is not being delivered physically, there is no need for a physical street address. The content begins with a salutation: "Dear Mr./Ms. Employer:" Since you are not able to sign an e-mail, type your name on the line following the closing.

An e-mail does not contain an envelope. Its first impression comes from the sender's e-mail address and the subject line. Any professional correspondence must come from a professional e-mail address. Something that may be enjoyable or a joke to you may not be appropriate for the job search. As with the résumé, remember that you are projecting your image to the potential employer. E-mail return addresses that include "watsamattau," "doughho," "tequilashooter04," or "Billythekid2009" do not sound professional. Create an e-mail account that contains your name or part of your name, something that can be readily associated with you. Change your settings so that the recipient sees your name or your name and e-mail address, rather than e-mail address alone. This creates the feeling that one individual is contacting another individual.

The subject line of your e-mail is the pitch to your pitch. A boring subject line, such as "Application" or "Hello Mr. Jones," or the ultimate insurance that your e-mail will be deleted—no subject line at all—does not really create any desire, interest, or urgency for the reader to open it. Think for a minute about some of the junk mail you receive. Have you ever noticed something marked "URGENT! OPEN IMMEDIATELY!" first in your inbox, and, even though it was spam, it held your attention? We are not suggesting that you use all caps and shout "URGENT!"; but rather you should establish a happy medium. "Professional Chef Seeking Opportunity," "Fellow Culinarian Seeking Advice," or "Good Morning, Mr. Jones" all create the feeling of an individual connecting with an individual.

Job Applications

Your résumé and cover letter are your primary self-marketing tools during the job search. The following section demonstrates how to put these tools into action as you seek out and apply for job opportunities.

At a job fair

Locating Jobs

Based upon your goals and your conversations with mentors and advisors, you may have established some job titles that you are looking to target. These are most likely going to be entry level or a bit higher; they require more skills than your foundational experience and are still positions of growth.

The first place to look for opportunities is on job boards such as Monster, Hot Jobs, or CareerBuilder. A good aggregate search engine, meaning that it pulls from many job boards and company Web sites, is Indeed. If you attended school, your school may have its own job board that you can take advantage of. Even though only about two in every ten available positions are posted or advertised, job boards are a good first step because they are valuable sources of information:

○ *These positions are available. Begin with, and take advantage of, obvious solutions.*

○ *You can see job descriptions, requirements, and desired characteristics, giving you the immediate ability to customize your application to the specific employer. You can also assume that similar positions with other employers will have the same requirements, allowing you to customize your application materials for the purpose of prospecting nonposted positions.*

○ *You can see who is hiring, and how frequently. Does the same employer post the same positions every week? This might indicate high turnover.*

○ *You have an immediate point of contact. The advertisement will tell you how they want you to apply. Follow their directions.*

○ *You can keep this information for future use. Many employers advertise opportunities and give points of contact for applicants on their Web sites and social media applications. If you have identified specific employers, search their sites first.*

Applying for Posted Positions

The advertisement will instruct you how to apply for the position. Follow these directions completely. "Send statement of interest, salary requirements, and résumé within the body of an e-mail to:" is not a guideline; it is a definitive set of instructions. This is a test of each applicant's ability to follow directions. Applicants who cannot follow directions are not considered. If an application form is required, either on paper or online, fill out this form completely. If the information is on your résumé, fill out the form completely and provide your résumé.

During the course of your application process, you may be directed to "apply online," which may include a form and the option to submit your résumé and cover letter. Applications submitted in this way are generally processed by applicant tracking system (ATS) software. This means that your application is judged by a computer program before it is seen by a human. It allows companies to efficiently receive and process enormous amounts of applications and to save, correlate, and produce data.

The parameters for successful candidates are set in advance. The list of responsibilities and desired and preferred qualifications and skills are the criteria the software uses to judge applications. Work through your résumé and cover letter to match up as many of the phrases, word for word, for these desired characteristics as possible. The software searches exact words.

The following sample entry-level position listing is taken from an advertisement for an entry-level cook, from a large company that uses an ATS.

"Prepare ingredients for cooking, including portioning, chopping, and storing food. Wash and peel fresh fruits and vegetables. Weigh, measure, and mix ingredients. Prepare and cook food according to recipes, quality standards, presentation standards, and food preparation checklist. Prepare cold foods. Operate ovens, stoves, grills, microwaves, and fryers. Test foods to determine if they have been cooked sufficiently. Monitor food quality while preparing food. Setup and break down work station . . . "

Sample entry-level position listing

Notice the word choices. *Prepare* appears three times. *Standards* is mentioned twice, as is *quality*. Repetition of words is a clear indication that these exact words are important to have on your application. The program searches for exact matches. If you were to reply to this ad, the word *prepare* would be a more appropriate choice to use on your résumé than *cook*. Likewise, *according to standards* is more appropriate than *as directed*.

The directions to apply for this entry-level position on-line are:

"Click on 'Apply Now, United States and Territories — Non-Management,' which will open a new window. Upon entering the application Web site, search for openings by zip code. Then click 'Submit.' Click the 'View Open Positions and Apply' link to be taken to a list of departments with open positions. On the department page, select the appropriate department and then the open positions in that department will appear. From there, click 'Apply Now' and begin filling out the entire application until you receive a message indicating your completion."

In this particular posting, the company name and recruiter's contact information do appear; however, this person will not respond to applications if contacted directly. The posting even instructs that there will be a prompt indicating successful completion of the application; if that is not received, the application is not complete.

When the posting lists specific skill sets, as this example does, it is easy to adjust your résumé to match those tangible skills. But how does one handle less concrete skills, such as: "Candidates must be willing to dedicate themselves to their craft;" "We employ cooks who love what they do in an enjoyable workplace;" and "Must be professional with an awesome attitude"? These are attitudes, not skills, so this information will not appear on your résumé. However, you can demonstrate this attitude within your cover letter with effective storytelling. At this point in your career, your skill level is not yet your greatest asset; in actuality, the skill set of a novice may be viewed as a detriment because of the perceived amount of training required. Your greatest asset is your passion, your drive to increase your knowledge and skills.

Tell a story with your cover letter to demonstrate this passion. One method that works well is to relate why you have chosen to do what you do. This shows that you care about what you do and how you connect with your job; you are not just a mercenary out for a paycheck. Offer examples to demonstrate self-motivation, times when you went after opportunities on your own and beyond your assigned duties in order to gain more skill, experience, or education. This shows you take responsibility for your own advancement rather than waiting to follow directions. Employers can train to increase skill level, but they cannot train someone to want to do the job and want to do it well.

Prospecting

Applying to posted, open positions is straightforward as long as you have the appropriate contact information, a description of the position, and some information about desired qualifications for that position. This type of application is a sales task for which you know the "customer" wants a "product," and your goal is to make them want your product (you).

Prospecting is still a sales task, with the added challenge of convincing the "customer," who may not be in the market for a "product," that they actually do need a product, and moreover, that they need your product.

First, you need to identify potential employers. Use your network, Internet search engines, publications, travel reviews, and so on to identify potential employers. Look for companies and businesses with a mission that is in line with your long-term goals. For instance, you may have a long-term goal to become an event planner. Where do wedding planners work? A search for "event planners" will yield some companies; however, if your experience at this point is food-related, you may not have had the breadth of experience yet to apply directly to these companies. Caterers, hotels, and resorts host weddings, parties, and gatherings. Applying to these types of establishments in a kitchen or service role will get you in the door, and once there, you will be in a position to establish a relationship with the event sales team, and build your event planning skills at the same time that you are building your culinary experience.

Perhaps you have a long-term goal of working in a management capacity. You have some culinary experience and a bachelor's degree with a management focus. Without management experience, however, you are not a viable candidate for even an entry-level position. How do you gain

A recruiter for a national hotel chain recently visited seventeen culinary and hospitality schools to recruit their bachelor's students. The recruiter had only thirty available Manager-in-Training positions, but she also had more than 1,000 positions the students could apply for that would give them the opportunity to grow into a management position within the company. She noted that many candidates make the mistake of only applying for one of the few MIT positions and getting discouraged if they do not get that job. Her candid advice: Get into the company in any capacity, and grow from within.

Don't Block Yourself In

the experience to get the job when you need experience to get the very job you need to gain that experience? A management training program is one option. Another option is to apply for a position with a company that offers the opportunity for growth into managerial positions. This strategy provides you with the opportunities to learn the what and how of the company's business, to create contacts within the company who will serve as internal references, and to demonstrate your benefit to the company directly.

Job Prospects

Whether actively looking for a job or not, it is important to remember that we are all job seekers — there is very little security that any given job will be available tomorrow. To prepare for an imminent, future, planned, or unforeseen change in employment, having a running list of job prospects is a useful tool. When actively applying for jobs, record every communication — people you spoke with, the name and address of the establishment, and contact information, as well as dates. Save copies of all correspondence. When you speak with someone, summarize the conversation and store your notes in the appropriate subfolder in your career filing cabinet.

There will be times when you are contacting a potential employer but you do not know whether there are any openings. This is called a "prospecting letter." An opening may be worded like this: "I am a culinary professional who seeks to bring my skills, experience, and education to your service team." In this example, the writer is not specifying an exact position, but rather a specific area. This shows direction, as the writer is not looking for just any available opportunity, yet it still leaves the door open to several possibilities.

A prospecting letter would highlight your skills as a reflection of the type of job you are looking to obtain. Looking for a position in the kitchen? Highlight that you can cook. Looking for sales? Highlight ways that you have grown and increased business through effective prospecting, demonstration, and customer service. Looking to teach? Highlight your abilities as a coach and mentor.

If you are not actively pursuing new opportunities, use this subfolder to house information on interesting companies, interesting people, and so on. You never know when that information may come in handy.

More Education or Training

If you are already working in a culinary career and want to make a move to the next level, you may be considering a higher degree in education. You should start considering your options early, because earning a degree takes time, especially if you are working. Read the job descriptions for the position you want and take particular note of the education requirements. Some items will be required, while others may be preferred. Some jobs will specify the area of study needed, and some may simply ask for a specific education level (such as a bachelor's or master's).

Use resources like LinkedIn to learn more about people who have positions to which you aspire. You will be able to learn more about the degrees they have and the schools they attended. Now you are ready to start comparing programs and schools. You will learn about entrance requirements for those schools, tuition costs, and how long it typically takes to complete the degree. You can also find out whether there are online options, as well as requirements for residencies, internships, practicums, licenses, and more. Keep the results of your research in your "Education" folder.

Establishing Initial Contact

After having identified potential employers, thoroughly research them, as discussed previously. Look for a point of contact. Sometimes the Web site may provide the names of the management team (chef, general manager, owner, and so on), and there is often a "Contact Us" option. This information can be used to address your cover letter to a specific person. If you are unable to find this level of information, go directly to the source. Call the establishment. At this point, we caution against asking to speak with the hiring manager or asking if they are hiring. This is called a "cold call." It is very easy for the person to say "No" and hang up. Your goal is rather to gain information. Call and say something like, "I am trying to e-mail [person], could you please confirm the spelling of his name and e-mail?" If that does not work, try calling on another day at another time;

someone else may answer the phone and be more willing to speak. If all else fails, send a hard copy of your résumé and cover letter through the mail.

Arriving in person to deliver a résumé is another cold-calling tactic. This can be more effective than calling on the phone; it is easy to dismiss an impersonal call but much harder to dismiss someone standing in front of you. **If you choose to approach a potential employer in person, keep the following in mind:**

○ *Visit the establishment during down times, not during service.*

○ *Arrive dressed as you would be at the start of a workday: clean, pressed, professional.*

○ *Carry a professional portfolio or notebook (as opposed to a folder) with copies of your résumé and cover letter printed.*

○ *If you are turned away without being able to speak with anyone, do not argue or show disappointment. Leave your résumé and cover letter. Ask the person you are speaking with for their name, and thank them, by name, for their time. Write down the person's name as soon as you leave the building. This will come in handy later.*

The Importance of Follow-Up

A district manager for a broad line foodservice distributor shares this statistic while training new hires: For every five doors you knock on, one person will answer. For every five people who answer the door, one will listen to your pitch. For every five people who listen to your pitch, one person will buy something from you. According to this, it takes twenty-five cold calls to make one sale. Prospecting for a job can be thought of in a similar way. As of this writing, it is still a "buyer's market," meaning there are more candidates than available jobs. There are an infinite number of reasons why a potential employer may not respond (favorably or at all) to an inquiry from a job seeker. As frustrating as it is, as a job seeker, you must come to terms with the fact that not everyone will respond to you.

If you knock on a door and wait for a response, you may be waiting for a long time. If you knock on a door and, receiving no response, you move on, you have eliminated the possibility of making your pitch. If you are able to give your pitch and then wait for a response, again you may be waiting for a long time.

Convincing a potential employer that: a) they need to hire someone, and b) that someone is you, usually takes more than one attempt. It will likely demand repeated attempts and follow-ups. Every time you are able to engage a potential employer, you are increasing your chances of being hired. Effective follow-up is not pestering or stalking, although there are times when you do need to walk the line between assertion and annoyance. To continue with the sales metaphor, imagine a salesperson pitching to a highly desirable purchasing-manager client but who keeps getting turned away. The salesperson arrives each day and delivers the same pitch. Chances are good that the only effect the salesperson is having on the potential client is to annoy him or her. What if that same salesperson varied the approach by spacing out contact times, offering different ways the product can benefit the client, bringing different samples to display, or by talking with other employees besides the purchasing manager to create a buzz for the product? This salesperson has not guaranteed a sale by any means; however, he or she has created more opportunity to demonstrate the benefit of the product, and more benefits start to make better sense to the potential client.

After sending or dropping off a résumé, wait a week before following up. You have to assume that returning contact from an unsolicited application is not the top priority for a potential employer. If you have not heard back, call. Since you have already contacted the potential employer, this is no longer a cold call; it is a warm call. You now have something to talk about. Let them know you sent your résumé and that you are following up to see if they have received it. If they have, ask to arrange for a time to discuss your application. If they have not, confirm their e-mail address and send another copy immediately. Perhaps you connect to voice mail, or someone offers to take a message instead of putting you in contact with the correct person. Remember to be polite and positive. Even a little frustration is easily detected in the voice, and this can be a turnoff to a potential employer.

How long should you continue to follow up before focusing your efforts elsewhere? The answer really depends on you. **It is probably time to look elsewhere if:**

○ *At any point, you are focusing all of your efforts to contact one potential employer and not considering prospecting for other opportunities.*

○ *You have tried on several occasions and with varied methods (e-mail and phone; at different times of day on different days of the week; by letter and in person).*

○ *You are becoming increasingly annoyed, and it may be showing. This does not mean that you have to give up your dream of working for a specific employer; it means that you need to be smart with your job search. A "no" or nonresponse now does not mean forever. You can shift your immediate focus toward other options and still occasionally look to connect with that dream employer.*

Summary

In this chapter we have explored creating your primary self-marketing tools, your résumé and cover letter, and how to put these tools to practical use when applying for a job. Résumés and cover letters are not one-size-fits-all items. By understanding their functionality, usefulness, and purpose, they can be shaped to best suit their audience. Like an amuse-bouche, their goal is to present a summary of your skills, experience, and potential benefit in one small bite that leaves the reader wanting more.

Putting the résumé and cover letter to good use is the job seeker's goal. The job seeker first must locate potential opportunities, and then decide how best to approach potential employers. Applying for a job does not end with submitting a résumé or filling out an application. Job seekers need to actively follow up with potential employers if they are to move to the next stage, the interview, which is the focus of the next chapter.

Exercise

Writing a Cover Letter

Practice writing an introductory letter. Think of a job you want — today, tomorrow, or twenty-five years from now. Research this job to find an employer and a person to whom you could send the letter. Using the information you have learned in this chapter, compose a letter that answers these questions: What job am I applying for? Why do I want to work for you? Why should you hire me? After you have written your letter, read it aloud. Record yourself if possible. Listen to that recording and ask yourself: Would I look at that person's résumé?

four

LANDING A JOB: INTERVIEWING AND NEGOTIATING

YOU HAVE ALREADY PUT A TREMENDOUS AMOUNT of time and energy into creating your résumé and other promotional materials, researching potential employers, and attempting to connect with those employers. All of this work pays off when you are called in for an interview. An interview is an interaction in which both you and the employer have the opportunity to ask and answer questions to determine whether you are a proper fit for each other. Interviews are a single-elimination game; only the best candidates progress to the next round and receive offers. Interviewing is a skill that takes practice.

In this chapter, we discuss interviewing best practices and provide insight into some commonly asked interview questions. If the purpose of submitting an application is to get an interview, then the purpose of having an interview is to receive a job offer. We provide information that will assist you with managing offers, negotiating salary, accepting or respectfully declining offers, and constructive ways of moving forward if an offer is not received.

The Purpose of an Interview

Securing an interview is the goal of submitting an application for employment. When you are contacted for an interview, you can presuppose that you have the basic qualifications that the employer is looking for. Employers simply do not waste time interviewing candidates if they are not convinced of their qualifications. Getting called for an interview does not guarantee you have the position. You can be assured that there are other candidates with similar qualifications who are also in the running. The interview is your time to convince that employer that you are a better package than the other candidates.

If the cover letter was your pitch and the résumé your short commercial, then the interview is your infomercial — your opportunity to spend extended time interacting with your audience. There are two key words here: *extended* time, not unlimited time, and *interacting*, which means that the interview should be a dialogue. Let us be clear: The whole job search is a sales task, and the interview is your opportunity to close that sale.

Preparing for an Interview

Interviewing is a skill that takes practice. Many feel uncomfortable in interviews. This is natural. You want something (this job), you are being judged by a stranger, and you do not know (for the most part) who makes up your competition. There are many unknowns. Preparation can help remove some of this stress, or at least dial it back to a more manageable level.

At the time you applied for the position, you should have already familiarized yourself with the employer to some extent. However, before you go on the interview, it is time to dig even deeper.

Learning about the Position

Familiarize yourself with the job for which you are applying. Write down the list of responsibilities and the list of desired qualifications, if available. Maybe this position was not posted, or there was not a lot of detail given in the posting. In that case, research other, similar jobs to find more information. Search job boards or use your favorite search engine. Talk to some people in similar positions to find out what they do and what qualifications they have.

Set this list side by side with your résumé. Are there similarities? Now you have a list of strengths.

You may notice an item on the job list that you have done at another job, or perhaps in a volunteer capacity. If you have not already included it in your résumé, see if you can rewrite your résumé to include it.

Reword your résumé as necessary to match the exact phrasing of the qualities listed in the ad or job posting. This is your opportunity to show that you can speak in their language.

Your research may also turn up some qualifications or skills that you do not possess. These are your weaknesses. Make note of them so that you can be prepared to talk about them directly. We discuss how to address weaknesses during an interview on page 121.

The Business or Company

Turn your attention to the employer to find out who they are and how they do what they do. Even if you have already done this as you wrote your résumé and cover letter, now is the time to go deeper. Start with their Web presence to get a sense of how they are presenting themselves.

○ *What is the first thing you see when you pull up the site?*

○ *How does that first impression make you feel?*

○ *Are there pictures?*

_____

○ *Are there people in the pictures?*

_____

○ *What are they wearing?*

_____

○ *Is the text providing straightforward information, or is it providing information by crafting a story?*

_____

Answering these questions will help you understand how the company is presenting itself to the public and therefore how they expect their employees to present themselves.

What information are they providing? Information on their Web site or social networking pages is information they want the public to know. Do they have the following:

_____

○ *A mission statement?*

_____

○ *A philosophy?*

_____

○ *A focus?*

_____

○ *Awards?*

_____

○ *Recent press?*

_____

○ *Team or employee highlights (especially upper-level members)?*

_____

○ *Links to other like-minded businesses?*

_____

Go even deeper to find out what they do and who makes up their audience. Plug their name in to the search engine of your choice and see what comes up.

○   *Who is their competition?*

○   *What kind of attention are they getting in the press or other media?*

○   *Are there advertisements?*

Visit LinkedIn's Web site and plug in the company name. If you find any current or past employees, there may be additional information about the company that you can glean, including typical career progression, education level of current or former employees, and how long employees stayed with the company.

If they have a social networking presence, you can learn more about how they interact with their customers. Look at social sites to see if any of the company's team members (and especially the person who might be interviewing you) have a social or professional networking presence of their own.

○   *How many followers do they have?*

○   *Do their followers interact on their page, or is it strictly one-way communication?*

○   *Can you see their pages, groups, movies, music, friends?*

Connect with your network and find out if anyone either has worked for the company you are interested in or might know who has worked for the company. If you find someone, ask about the job, the environment, the people, advancement, business levels, and so on.

If possible, go to the establishment ahead of time. You can learn a number of important things that can make the actual day of the interview easier and more comfortable for you.

○   *How do you get there?*

○   *How long does it take?*

○ *Is there parking?*

_____

○ *What is the neighborhood like?*

_____

○ *Are you able to get past the lobby?*

_____

○ *Who is there?*

_____

○ *What do the employees and the customers they serve look like? Are they dressed formally or informally?*

_____

○ *Are the people friendly?*

_____

Call them up, around the same time of day as your interview (if possible, on the same day of the week).

_____

○ *Who answers the phone? This may be the first person you see when you arrive.*

_____

○ *Is this person friendly?*

_____

Take the answers to these preceding questions and interpret what you have learned.

_____

○ *What are they doing well?*

_____

○ *What is making them successful?*

_____

○ *What do you think are some challenges they are having; in other words, why is the job you are applying for open?*

_____

○ *What opportunities for positive changes are there?*

_____

You Can Sell:

	Old	New
Old	**Old (existing) products** TO **Old (existing) customers**	**New products** TO **Old (existing) customers**
New	**Old (existing) products** TO **New customers**	**New products** TO **New customers**

Ansoff Matrix

Write these answers down. The Ansoff Matrix is a useful way to communicate the value you will bring to the potential employer.

The Ansoff Matrix is a tool usually used to strategize product market growth. It says that there are old (current) customers and new (potential) customers. There are old (current) product offerings and new (potential) product offerings. You can sell old products to old customers; new products to old customers; old products to new customers; and the most challenging, new products to new customers. This way of thinking can be useful for an applicant to demonstrate his or her value to a potential employer. For instance, a sous chef is a management position. The sous chef must know how to cook and have a mind toward the business. A candidate for this position can view the menu, marketing materials, and reviews of a potential employer. The candidate can also research the competition. Through research, the candidate may notice that there is no late-night dining scene. This may be an opportunity to bring in new customers and more revenue. During the interview itself, the candidate can inquire about the menu mix, customer base, and current marketing strategies. The candidate can then offer further ideas on how to market existing and new menu items to existing and new guests.

You may be saying: "This is a lot of research. Aren't interviews about asking and answering questions?" Yes, the interview is an information-gathering conversation based in questions and answers. All of this research helps to focus the answers you will give and the questions you will ask. Think of all the information you have given that employer about you. They may have already searched your Web presence. They may have made some off-the-record calls about you. They will be coming prepared to the interview, and they expect that you will be prepared as well.

Etiquette

Often the word *etiquette* conjures up images of Miss Manners, high society, and the feeling of being constantly corrected for not following obscure rules that you do not understand. What is etiquette? Oxford Dictionary defines *etiquette* as "the customary code of polite behavior in society or among members of a particular profession or group." This definition narrows it down a bit. A bit more understanding is gained from Oxford Dictionary's definition of *polite*: "having or showing behavior that is respectful and considerate of other people." Etiquette, then, refers to the actual ways in which your behavior demonstrates your respect and consideration of others.

There are many wonderful resources that present social norms, expectations, and rules in great detail. This is an overview of some basic etiquette you should keep in mind as you apply and interview for a job, as well as suggestions to improve your social skills that are easy to implement and that will demonstrate your respect and consideration of others. If you act in a professional and courteous manner, then you are someone who can be taken seriously.

The saying is "You never have a second chance to make a first impression." This first impression, whether in person, in writing, by phone, or online, sets the tone for every subsequent encounter. As important as this initial point of contact is, the truth is that every point of contact creates an impression. The goal is to create a positive initial contact and carry that positive feeling throughout the relationship.

On a job interview

In Person

○ **Arrive on time.** *Tardiness demonstrates a lack of respect. Being late creates a negative environment before you even come through the door. If you are late during the job search, when you are presumably at your best, you are show-ing a potential employer how you will be once you have the job. Make a habit of using a calendar, entering all appointments, and reviewing your calendar both before you go to sleep and first thing in the morning. Look several days ahead to prepare for upcoming events. Set alarms and reminders. Know your-self. If you are not a morning person, do not schedule important meetings in the morning. Call to reschedule if you are running late.*

- *Dress appropriately. Your appearance "speaks" before you have the opportunity to say anything at all. In a job search situation, it is better to err on the side of formality, at least initially. A good rule is to dress for the position you want, even if that is not the job you are immediately pursuing. For kitchen positions, clean, pressed whites are appropriate — arrive as if you are ready to jump on the line (bring your tools as well). Remember that as an employee, you will be a representative of that company, a small part of something bigger. Dress the way that the guests, clients, and customers expect.*

- *Men: Business dress means a suit, with slacks, a long-sleeve oxford shirt, a tie, a jacket, a belt, and polished shoes. All clothes must be clean, pressed, and fitted, and the belt and shoes should match. Your socks should match the pants. Ties should break at the belt line, and the top button of the shirt must always be buttoned when wearing a tie. Wear minimal cologne, if any. "Business casual" means business dress without the tie and jacket. If you are wondering whether what you are wearing qualifies as business casual, it probably does not. A watch and wedding band are acceptable; earrings or other visible piercings and tattoos are most likely not.*

- *Women: Business dress means a suit, with slacks or a skirt, a shirt, and a jacket. Skirts should be knee length, and hosiery should be worn. No cleavage should be revealed. Wear closed-toe shoes with moderate heels, or flats. If you are not comfortable in heels, do not wear them on an interview. A watch, wedding band, one earring per lobe, bracelet, and necklace are appropriate, but other visible piercings or tattoos are not. Wear minimal perfume, if any.*

- *When meeting someone, smile, make eye contact, and shake hands. The webbing between your right thumb and index finger should meet the webbing of the other's right thumb and index finger. Apply moderate pressure and give one "pump." Stand up when introduced. Repeat the person's name.*

- *Be courteous with your speech. Use titles and last names (Mr. Smith, Ms. Smith, Chef Smith) until directed otherwise. "Good morning/afternoon/evening," "Please," "Thank you," and "Excuse me" demonstrate respect.*

○ **Listen actively,** *and use nonverbal communication to demonstrate engagement. Making eye contact, leaning slightly in, and offering a slight nod all show that you are listening; looking around, fidgeting, moving away, and crossing your arms in front of your chest indicate that you are distracted or closed off.*

○ **Turn off your cell phone** *to avoid the temptation to answer or view a message. Remove earphones.*

If a meal is a part of the interview process, remember that it is an interview, not an opportunity for sustenance. In addition to the questions, answers, and conversation, you are being judged on your interactions with the staff. Be polite and courteous to everyone—host, waitstaff, busser. Wait to sit until the host sits. Order food that is easy to eat, and minimize the potential for mess (long pasta with red sauce or the whole lobster may not be the best idea). Do not speak with your mouth full. Do not drink alcohol, even if others at the table are drinking.

Over the Phone

○ **Plan and prepare in advance.** *Charge your phone fully. Create a quiet space where you will not be disturbed and where you have good reception. Spread your résumé and any notes in front of you. This way you do not have to shuffle papers while holding the phone, minimizing background noise. If you are to call the other person, call at the time scheduled.*

○ **Ask to speak with the person you are calling and introduce yourself.** *If someone other than the person you are calling answers, and they give their name, address that person directly: "Good morning, Jonathan. This is Robert Smith calling. Is Ms. Jones available?" Remember to be courteous at all times — gatekeepers have the choice to put your call or message through, or not.*

- If the person you are calling is unavailable, and you have the opportunity, leave a message. *Leave your name, number, purpose of the call, and repeat your name and number. Frustration and anger come out in your voice, so be positive and matter of fact.*

- Think before you call. *What time zone are you calling? Is it an acceptable time to call (nine to five for businesses; avoid lunch and dinner service hours if calling a kitchen). Dress even for a phone conversation. Professional dress encourages a professional demeanor. Sit up straight or stand.*

- Think before you answer your phone. *If you are not in the position to take a call, do not answer. If you do answer, be polite and cheerful. Return messages promptly.*

- Have a professional outgoing message. *Having your name and number on your outgoing message lets the caller know they have reached the correct phone. Your favorite music or a joke may not be received well by a potential employer or professional contact.*

On Paper

- Be formal in all written communication. *Address the person professionally ("Dear Mr./Ms." or title if appropriate, and last name). Use a professional closing ("Sincerely" is appropriate). Proofread for correct capitalization at the beginning of each sentence and for proper nouns. Organize your thoughts into paragraphs. Do not use all caps, which creates the feeling of yelling, or large amounts of italics, which can be difficult to read. Spell words completely. Emoticons are never acceptable in professional communication.*

- Always include *a subject line when e-mailing.*

- Create a professional e-mail address. *As with your outgoing voice mail message, what is funny, cute, or clever to you may not be so to a professional contact.*

- **There is no need to introduce yourself ("My name is . . .") at the start of the letter.** *Your name will appear at the end of the letter. Written communication is different from verbal communication.*

- **Do not assume there will be a response.** *If you would like a response, let the reader know.*

- **It is good practice** *to close the letter or e-mail by thanking the reader for his or her time.*

- **If attaching an item to an e-mail, let the reader know what is attached and the program it is in.** *If at all possible, convert the attachment to a pdf file that can be opened across a variety of platforms and programs.*

- **If sending an application via e-mail, the body of the e-mail is the cover letter.** *Unless specifically stated otherwise, include your résumé as an attachment.*

Online

Connecting virtually does not diminish the need for professionalism. Potential and current employers, peers, and network contacts can search for you without your knowing and may make judgments based upon your Web presence.

- **Be conscious of and smart about your Web presence.** *Keep your privacy settings at the tightest level available. This does not guarantee that any information online is secure; however, it keeps the casual viewer away from your information. You may feel you have nothing to hide, but think of the message you are sending: If you cannot keep your own private information (birthday, opinions, and other things) private, can you be trusted to keep your employer's information private?*

- **Be aware of your profile picture.** *What are you doing and what are others doing in that picture? Does that picture disclose your race, gender, religion, national origin, or ethnicity?*

- **Use different applications for friends and professional contacts.** *Encourage professional contacts to connect with you on LinkedIn, for example, while reserving Facebook for your friends and family.*

- **When you send a request to connect, add a personalized message.** *Briefly let the person know why you are looking to connect.*

- **It is okay to turn down a request to connect.** *Refer the person elsewhere if possible. For instance, let a co-worker know that you use Facebook for friends and family and that you prefer to keep work connections on LinkedIn.*

- **Remember that everything you put online could be accessed, even without your permission.** *Your privacy settings may be secure; however, your friend's may not be as secure. If someone wants to find out about you, they probably can and will.*

When It All Goes Wrong

No matter how hard you try to be professional, you may slip up. You may unintentionally offend someone because you are unaware of another's cultural norms or another's individual life circumstances; you may forget a name; you may discover too late that there is a huge stain in plain view on your clothing; or you may be caught in traffic and become delayed for an initial meeting. If something goes wrong, acknowledge it, apologize, and take steps to rectify the situation. People take emotional cues from each other. Letting something obviously crush you will garner a different reaction than if you use humor or a sincere apology and move on. No one is perfect. You can only do your best to offer the same respect to others as you would like to receive from others.

Logistics

The interview is set. You have made arrangements to meet in person, over the phone, or via video. Now, make sure your mise en place is in order.

Face-to-Face Interviews

○ **Know where,** *when, and with whom you are meeting.*

○ **Do a dry run if possible.** *Understand the traffic for that time of day and the parking availability.*

○ **Have the interviewer's number** *with you and call if you are delayed.*

○ **Bring multiple copies of your résumé,** *your portfolio (if applicable), a professional notebook, notes from your research, a pen, and mints.*

○ **Arrive** *ten minutes early.*

○ **Turn off your cell phone,** *and keep it out of sight to remove the temptation to check messages.*

○ **Do not smoke before the interview.** *Do not smoke while wearing your interview clothes.*

○ **Have a breath mint** *before entering the building.*

○ **Be polite to everyone you encounter.** *Ask their names, and shake their hands. Say good-bye to them when you leave.*

Phone Interviews

- **Establish who will call whom,** *at what number, and the time.*

- **Establish a quiet space** *where you will not be disturbed.*

- **If using a cell phone,** *make sure you have an area where you get good reception, and have your phone fully charged.*

- **Have your résumé,** *notes, pen, and paper available.*

- **Dress as you would for a face-to-face interview** *(see Etiquette section, page 112, for tips on professional dress). This will encourage you to maintain a professional demeanor.*

- **Answer the phone professionally;** *for example, "Good morning, this is John Smith."*

Video Interviews

- **Establish who will contact whom** *and at what time.*

- **Establish a quiet space.** *Position the camera so that you can look at it naturally, as if you were in a face-to-face conversation.*

- **Dress as you would for a face-to-face interview** *(see Etiquette section, page 112, for tips on professional dress).*

- **Notice your surroundings** *— be aware of backlighting and the environment that can be seen around you.*

- Have a copy of your résumé, notes, paper, and pen available. *Spread out multiple pages of notes so they can be easily viewed without the noise of rustling pages.*

- Test your camera, microphone, and speakers *prior to the call.*

- Look at the camera, not the screen. *This mimics eye contact.*

- Sit up straight.

Interview Questions

Imagine an interview and you immediately think of questions— lots of questions. There are many categories of questions that an employer may ask, some easy to prepare for and others much more challenging. As you prepare for your interview, remember that for every question asked, you should have a ready answer that sells you into that position. The answers need to be truthful and focused. The interview may feel like a casual conversation, but it is not. You are selling a product. Your main goal in an interview is to secure the next point of contact. You want them to want to see you again, either in the next round of interviews or at the time clock on your first day.

There are some common questions, and common categories of questions, that are asked in interviews. Let's look at six examples.

- Tell me *about yourself.*

- What are your strengths *and weaknesses?*

- Why did you leave *(or why are you leaving) your last (or current) job?*

- Tell me about a time *when you had a conflict with a co-worker.*

○ **Tell me** *a joke.*

_____

○ **Do you have any questions** *for me?*

_____

Each of these items is representative of a category of information an employer is looking for. We have left out industry- and job-specific skill questions, but you should know they will be asked and be prepared to give thoughtful answers that show you understand what you are doing.

Tell me about yourself.

Overview: This question, or one similar to it, is usually the first one you will be asked. It gives both you and the interviewer an opportunity to grow a bit more at ease with each other. You should practice your answer a few times because there is more going on than simply getting to know you.

The employer is looking at how you communicate. You know they will ask this question. They know you know they will ask this question. You presumably know yourself better than anyone, so this should be the easiest subject to speak about. The employer is handing you an opportunity to create a connection and sell yourself into the position.

Pitfalls: The biggest pitfall here is being caught off guard by this question — you should have a brief and relevant answer prepared. This is not an opportunity to tell your complete life story, nor is it the question to answer with "Ummm." Your answer should be long enough to paint a picture of your professional history as it relates to the job at hand.

Best Practices: Create a summation of your professional experience in advance. Tell it as a story, a logical progression with some interesting details as opposed to a flat, verbal list or word-for-word recitation of your résumé. Use your experiences to make a connection to the employer or interviewer (remember all that research you did earlier?), and offer specific accomplishments that highlight the relevant skill sets required for this position.

Similar Questions: "Walk me through your résumé" and "Why should we hire you?"

What are your strengths and weaknesses?

Overview: Employers ask this question to find out about how you view yourself. In order to answer this question, you must be able to view yourself objectively. The employer can see how well you can separate personal judgments from work judgments. This is especially important for management and supervisory positions that include employee performance evaluation or discipline as part of the job.

Pitfalls: Candidates are sometimes unrealistic and imbalanced in their perceptions of themselves. Some candidates have great difficulty communicating their strengths, identifying and showing pride at those things they do well. Others feel they do many things exceptionally well.

If a candidate claims to have a large number of strengths and hardly any weaknesses, the employer may interpret that to mean that the candidate is overconfident and might not be willing to learn the employer's way of doing things. If a candidate appears to focus on weaknesses in or limits to their experience or training, the employer will interpret that to mean that the candidate will require much additional training. This forces the employer to consider whether they believe they will make back the investment needed to to bring the candidate up to their standard.

Best Practices: Create a list of three to five strengths and weaknesses as they relate to the particular job, using the list you created earlier while researching the position. Strengths should have supporting examples. For example, if "team-oriented" is in the job description, you would want to highlight this as a strength. Rather than saying, "I am a team player," you could respond, "I work well in a group setting to reach a common goal. At my last job, I assisted other stations when needed. I also knew when to ask for help and delegate responsibility. When we all worked together, we all stayed out of the weeds and put the food out to the guests within an appropriate time."

Everyone has weaknesses; they are only negatives if you allow them to be. Communicate all "weaknesses" in terms of opportunities for growth. This can be done by presenting them as positive goals. As people start to move up the ladder, their main weakness is that they do not have the titled experience in the job for which they are applying. Take this example: job requirement, 1 year of management experience; weakness, no titled management experience. Response: "Although I do not have the exact titled experience that the advertisement mentions, in my last position I effectively trained new hires, and suggested and implemented ways to increase sales, such as creating a drink-appetizer pairing for guests waiting for their tables at the bar. One of my goals with this position is to move this business forward. I am fully ready to contribute as I learn your systems and grow into the position."

Similar Questions: "How would your last/current supervisor describe you?" "What are your biggest successes/failures?" "Where do you want to be in five years?"

Why did you leave your last job?
Why are you leaving your current job?

Overview: Here is another question that seems to ask for a negative response. If you last/current job was great, why leave? The employer is looking for two things here: How are you going to speak about your past employer, which gives an indication of how you will speak about this employer; and what motivates you, which may indicate how long they can expect you to stay with this job.

Pitfalls: Honesty is always best; however, there is more than one way to be honest. Some candidates may fall into the trap and speak very negatively about their last job. On the other end of the spectrum, a candidate can be so overly positive that he or she is obviously hiding something, usually a termination. Worse than either of these two extremes is not having an answer at all.

Best Practices: Be honest and positive. Your boss may have been the worst SOB in the world whom you would not wish your most hated enemy to work for, but it is better not to say that. Instead, try a positive spin, such as "I learned and grew tremendously in that position, and I understood that I can flourish more and contribute more in a different type of environment." Or "There is limited opportunity for growth at my current position."

Termination is something that happens from time to time. Be straight-forward about the reasons you were terminated, and demonstrate that there has been a change. "I was terminated for talking back to my boss. It is really humiliating to be fired. It gave me the wake-up call that I needed to realize that I don't know everything, and that the way I was taught is not the only way to do something. Since then I have opened myself to understanding why things are done the way they are done, and I have grown to understand that there are more appropriate ways to make suggestions, and that it is okay to agree to disagree."

Similar Questions: "What did you like best/least about your last job?" "Describe your favorite/least favorite supervisor." "Have you ever been terminated?"

Tell me about a time when you had a conflict with a supervisor.

Reason: The "tell me about a time . . ." questions are called "behavioral questions." Rather than give hypothetical situations and ask you to come up with a solution, these questions ask you to give an example of how you handled the situation in the past, with the theory that past action is indicative of future action. The employer is looking for specifics: a specific situation, how you handled it, and the outcome.

Pitfall: Not having specifics. The employer wants to understand your process when encountering a difficult situation. Sometimes the candidate may not have been in the exact situation the question asks about, and may fail to give any information.

Best Practices: These types of questions generally revolve around conflicts — with supervisors, co-workers, and/or guests. Think of times when you had a conflict with each. State specifically what the situation was, the specific steps you took to resolve the situation, and the results of your actions. The results may not have always been positive or what you would have liked them to be. In that case, also describe what you learned from the situation and how you know that you can handle it better the next time.

If the question does not specifically fit a situation you have directly experienced, modify the question and give the same situation, steps toward resolution, and outcome answer that the employer is looking for. For example: "Tell me about a time when you had a conflict with your supervisor." Your response could be: "I have been lucky not to have had any major conflicts with supervisors, but there was a situation with a co-worker . . ."

Similar Questions: Anything that begins with "Tell me about a time . . ." or "Describe for me . . ."

Tell me a joke.

Reason: There are some questions that you can never anticipate and therefore never plan for. If you encounter these types of questions, remember that the employer is not interested in your answer as much as they are interested in your reaction to the question and how you answer. Employers may purposefully try to throw you off, antagonize you, and make you uncomfortable to see how you would handle yourself on the job. Many situations arise where you are called upon to make a difficult decision, to deliver news or an action that you may not personally believe is right, or to handle a situation where the other party is upset or truly out of line. The employer is testing to see if you will remain calm and in control during a stressful situation.

Pitfalls: Displaying surprise, worry, anger, or confusion. When a situation is stressful and you are charged with being the voice of reason or the face of the company, it is of the utmost importance that you are not swayed by the emotion of the other party.

Best Practices: Roll with the question. Know that it is there to throw you off. Remain composed and professional at all times (no off-color jokes in response to the question above!), and do your best to answer the question in the spirit in which it was asked.

Similar questions: "Why are manhole covers round?" "How many gas stations are there in LA?" "If you could have dinner with anyone, who would it be?"

One interviewer is known to ask the same question twice in a row: "What is your biggest accomplishment?" followed immediately by "What is your biggest accomplishment?"

Do you have any questions for me?

Reason: This question usually is one of the last questions of the interview. The interviewer is giving you the opportunity to bring up any topics that may not have been covered during the conversation. Ideally, you will have been asking questions during the whole interview.

Pitfalls: Not having any questions; asking questions that are easily answered by looking at a Web site or through a basic understanding of the company; asking about salary or benefits during an initial interview.

Best Practices: Remember that you are interviewing the company as much as they are interviewing you. Create some questions ahead of time that will help you gain a thorough understanding of the expectations of the specific job, the expectations of employees in general, and the environment in which you will be working. Questions like "Describe a typical day/week for me;" "Describe for me your most successful employee in this position;" and "What brought you here, and what keeps you here?" are all open-ended questions that will get the interviewer talking and give you a better understanding of the work environment. The employer's answers during the interview can give you insight into how you should answer his or her questions as well.

These six categories of questions, in some shape or form, will be asked in almost every interview. Take some time to prepare answers in advance. Have a friend ask you the questions, so that you are forced to verbalize the answer. Alternatively, record yourself (a webcam is ideal) answering these questions. Watch yourself, or have your friend watch how you answer the questions. Do you keep appropriate eye contact? Do you use the same words over and over? Are you fidgety? Do you use verbal pauses ("um" and "like")? It is okay to be a bit nervous and to be yourself during an interview; however, it is best to understand ahead of time if you do have any habits or actions that may distract and detract from your presentation to the potential employer.

As you prepare for your interview, it is important to understand the different roles of the people you may be interviewing with. There are times when you will initially meet with a recruiter or human resources representative before meeting with the actual hiring manager or supervisor. An HR rep may ask questions focusing on your fit with the company itself, whereas the hiring manager or direct supervisor will ask questions more focused on the actual job you will be doing.

Ending the Interview

Ending the interview is as important to your success as every other element of the interview. Remember your goal: to obtain a next point of contact. Every time you have contact with that employer, you have another chance to demonstrate that you are the right person for this job. Ultimately that next point of contact could be your first day on the job. If you are still interested in the position at the end of the interview, let the employer know that. It is professional to say, "I enjoyed our conversation and look forward to joining your team." Before you leave the room, hang up the phone, or end the video chat, *establish the next point of contact*! Building on the last sentence, you can follow with: "I am sure you are considering other candidates. I would like to connect with you again next week to see if I can supply any additional information you may need from me. Can we schedule a time on Thursday for a five-minute follow-up call? In the meantime, I would like to send you an invitation to connect on LinkedIn. May I do that?" Now there is no uncomfortable and stressful waiting to see if they will call you, no wondering if you should call them, and no worrying about why they are not calling. You have scheduled your follow-up, and even if there is not an answer at that time, you have another opportunity to promote yourself for the position. Before ending the interview, collect everyone's contact information, and make sure everyone has a copy of your résumé.

After the Interview

Following any interview, schedule some time to review and reflect upon what has transpired. Make some notes: What questions did they ask? What were your answers? What information did you find out? Looking at these notes, is there anything you wish you had said differently or are there questions you did not ask at the time? List the people you met and some notes about each to help you identify them when you meet them again.

Send a thank-you note as soon as possible. Since we live in an electronic world, this can be done almost instantly. Thank the interviewers for their time, reiterate that you are interested in the position, highlight one or two of your strongest points, and confirm that next point of contact that you established. If you have any further questions or any further information you would like to clarify, briefly include it in this communication.

An additional, brief, thank-you letter or card can be sent via snail mail. A handwritten card adds a personal focus that can set you apart from other candidates. The follow-up e-mail is an expectation; a tangible personalized card or letter is a bonus.

Obtaining an Offer

We advise against focusing on salary during the early stages of the job search, in favor of obtaining information about the position to learn whether it is a correct fit for you. Assuming that both you and the employer are prepared to go to the next step, you can be certain that, at some point, salary will be discussed.

It is often said in business that the party who talks the most loses, meaning that by talking one party is giving information to the other. This saying applies to salary negotiation as well: The first to name a price loses. Keep in mind that the employer already has a budgeted range for every position. They know how much they are willing to pay. As discussed previously, if providing salary expectations is a requirement of the application process, you must provide this information to be considered for the position. **If the employer asks directly during the interview process, depending upon your**

level of confidence in your research and your ability to do the job, here are some possible responses:

○ *"Before discussing salary, I would like to discuss more about the responsibilities and your expectations of the position to see if I would be a good fit."*

○ *"Based on my research, salaries for this type of position in this area begin in the mid to upper $___. Is that the range you had in mind?"*

○ *"I understand that you have a range budgeted for this position. Let's look at this range and do a side-by-side comparison of my qualifications versus the job requirements to decide where on that spectrum I would fall."*

Viewing the Total Offer

Even if a salary figure is said and verbally agreed upon, remember that in order to be valid, the offer *must be in writing!* There are no exceptions to this rule. Placing an offer in writing benefits both the candidate and the employer, because the expectations are clearly spelled out, and, once accepted, are legally binding. It is in your best interest as a candidate to request all offers in writing *and* to take some time to review any offer. If you are given a verbal offer, it is professional and acceptable to say something like: "Thank you for your offer. Before I make a decision, would you please send me an e-mail [or give me a hard copy] of the offer so that I can make sure that I am correctly understanding all the components of your offer?"

With the written offer in hand, it is time to weigh all the components in order to make a decision. You will have three choices: 1) accept the offer as is; 2) attempt to negotiate some of the components of the offer (in which case, you hope, another offer will be generated and you will complete another decision-making process); 3) decide against negotiating and respectfully decline the offer. No matter your answer, this is a decision that should not be made lightly. It is expected that you should take some time to consider any offer.

In order to make the best decision for you, review the following:

○ **What is the salary offered?** *Remember that this is a gross number, without taxes or other deductions. It is not your actual take-home pay. Is this number in line with your expectations, and does it allow you to meet your financial obligations? Is this an hourly or salaried position? If hourly, have you discussed overtime? (Generally, hourly employees are paid at one-and-a-half times their regular pay for hours worked over forty hours per week. Check with the regulations of your individual state. Employers are expected to comply with state laws, but we advise you not to assume anything.) If salaried, have you discussed the number of hours you are expected to work? Is the pay period weekly or biweekly?*

○ **Are there other elements of compensation besides money,** *such as insurance, paid time off, retirement contributions, stock options, extended disability, relocation assistance, meals, uniforms, child care, use of facilities, or tuition or continuing education assistance? These items will not show up in your check; however, they are items of value. Note that some elements, such as insurance and retirement, require both the employee and employer to contribute.*

○ **Does the position make sense for your career growth?** *Will you gain valuable skills and experience? Are there opportunities for advancement within the company? Is this a "recognized" company or position that will be beneficial for your future growth?*

○ **Does the position make sense for your overall well-being?** *Are the expectations of the position in line with the effort you are prepared to invest? Will this position allow you to better focus upon other areas of your life? Do you get a positive feeling from the people and environment at the establishment?*

○ **Have you spoken with your mentor** *or other trusted individuals about the position, the overall career benefit it may provide, and the fairness of the compensation package?*

Accepting the Offer As Is

If you are electing to accept the offer as it stands, do so *in writing*. Some companies' formal offer letters have a section where you can sign to accept or decline. If this is not the case, create a document or e-mail stating your intention to accept the position. Reiterate the terms, including expected start date, and provide your acceptance to the employer. You should absolutely also speak with the employer — you are entering into a happy relationship. Face-to-face (or at least verbal) contact is always best. The benefits of also accepting in writing mirror the benefits of having the offer in writing: Both parties have a concrete document outlining the specifics of the employee-employer relationship.

Perhaps the offer is generally good, but not quite what you had in mind. You would like to see if you can more closely align the terms of the offer with your expectations. Now is the time for negotiation. (See Negotiation Strategies, page 133, for more information on how to negotiate an offer.)

Managing Multiple Offers

Applying for multiple opportunities at the same time means that you may be faced with a challenge: choosing between multiple offers. This is a good problem to have because it demonstrates that your skills, experiences, and job search strategies have made you a desirable commodity. The goal is to select the position that best suits your needs while maintaining a positive relationship with the other employers that you turn down.

When you applied for these positions, perhaps you built a chart or spreadsheet to compare the potential positions to each other and to your needs/goals. If not, be sure to do this as the offers come in. Respond immediately to each offer, indicating that you have received it and appreciate the offer. If you are not prepared to accept it right away, communicate to the potential employer that you would like some time to consider the offer and provide a date for when you will follow up: "Thank you for offering me a position with your team. I would like to take some time to fully consider your offer. Could I connect with you again in two weeks, on May 14, with a firm answer?"

The employer may or may not give the time you ask for, which may force you to speed up your decision process. Once you have received multiple offers, compare what is being offered by each employer, as well as what is offered versus what was initially discussed. (Remember that everything must be in the written offer to be valid. If you discussed an item that does not appear in the offer, do not assume you will get that item.) Then compare all of these with your needs and goals.

Accept your top choice in writing, and politely decline all other offers. Employers are understanding when an offer is declined, as neither side has lost anything. Issues arise when a candidate accepts an offer, then backs out, or if an offer is made and there is no immediate response. Be aware that in either of these two cases, the candidate has severely hurt his or her chances of working for that employer in the future.

Declining an Offer

The offer as given or after negotiation may not meet your needs or expectations. This may be disappointing; however, remember that if you have received an offer, you have something that employer wants. This offer for this position is not going to work right now, but you may wish to revisit the idea of working for that employer (under different terms) at some point in the future. To this end, you want to keep a positive relationship with that company.

As with accepting, declining an offer should be done both in a verbal conversation and in writing. Remain positive in your language, and set the stage for the future by stating something like: "After careful consideration, I am unable to accept your offer at this time. I would like to remain in contact with you, and perhaps the future will provide another opportunity to work together."

Handling Rejection

Rejection is something that almost everyone experiences during a career. Even the most successful people have faced rejection. Being rejected is never anyone's goal, and learning how to minimize the negative effects of rejection will lead to greater success.

- **Control what you can control.** *It is within your ability to put together a great application and to be thoroughly prepared for an interview.*

- **Recognize that you cannot control everything.** *Other candidates may have been better qualified, the person who got the job may like the same baseball team as the hiring manager, or the company may have had to interview external candidates even though they knew they were going to hire an internal candidate. You cannot control these things, and you may never know why you were not chosen.*

- **Be honest with yourself.** *There is always someone more qualified than you are. If you applied for a position that you were not really qualified for, you are not a failure or bad person; you are just not ready yet.*

- **Recognize that you have not lost anything.** *In fact, every time you apply for a job, you gain something. It is only when you fail to act that you lose out.*

Handling Indifference

Rejection is difficult, but at least you know where you stand. If you submit an application and hear nothing, you are in a kind of limbo. Some companies are so overwhelmed with applicants for a single position that they feel they can only contact applicants who have the highest chance of success. Whether you agree with that policy or not, the fact is that sending résumés out into the world and never hearing back is difficult to take.

You have to judge how much time and effort you will spend on employers who are not returning your communications. Tenacity and persistence are good up to a point, after which they become time thieves. If you have tried to connect with a potential employer several times, via several different methods, at varied times of the day, then it may be time to redirect your efforts in a different direction.

Indifference is rarely worth taking personally. Do not let rejection and indifference shut you down. Continue to apply to other jobs and work toward your goals.

Negotiation Strategies

The end goal of any negotiation is to create a win-win situation. You are receiving compensation and working conditions you find fair, and the employer is receiving someone who will benefit (that is, increase the profitability of) the business. Employment should be a positive relationship. Keep this goal in mind as you negotiate. Consider the following items as you prepare to negotiate the terms of the offer.

- **Are you speaking with the correct person?** *It is a waste of time to discuss compensation with someone who does not have any authority to alter the terms of the offer. Speaking directly with the decision maker will ensure that your reasons are presented accurately and that you will receive a definite answer most expeditiously.*

- **Are you in a position to negotiate?** *Do your experience and skills exceed the requirements of the job, or are you selling them on your potential? Are you 100 percent certain you can meet and exceed additional expectations? (More compensation equals higher expectations of return on investment.)*

- **Based on your research, is your counteroffer reasonable?** *Are you keeping within the range of the position, taking into account the location, size, and type of the company? For example, a national chain may pay one range for a given position, regardless of geographical location (and the location's cost of living), so there may not be any room for negotiation.*

- **Are you approaching the discussion with multiple solutions?** *If wage cannot be changed, can schedule, insurance, time off, or other benefits be altered? Would the employer be willing to commit to a performance and wage review after sixty or ninety days? Will the employer outline a guideline for growth within the company so that you have an understanding of the opportunities for advancement during your tenure?*

- Are you prepared to continually highlight the benefits you bring to the employer, *demonstrating that you are going to immediately contribute to their business?*

- Are you prepared to accept if an agreement is made? *Negotiation should be a conversation. Ultimately, if you do not ask for what you feel is fair, you have no chance of receiving it. Remain positive throughout the discussion, and keep focusing the employer on the benefits you will bring to them.*

Folder: Salary Research

Unlike your salary history, salary research is aimed at finding out what the industry standards are for a position. These standards usually are given as ranges to account for the fact that years of experience, education, and geographic location have an impact on what employers are likely to pay.

- Do a Web search for job postings from the company to see if they have listed a salary or salary range for this position. If they have not, have they listed salary ranges for any other position? You can make some assumptions if you find a range for another position within the same company. Gauge the level of that position compared with the one you are applying for, and you can make an estimation from there.

- Do a Web search for similar positions within the same general area and see what other employers are paying. Using a free salary wizard site, search for a position in a specific area (city or zip code). They may not have the exact position; however, you can usually find a good approximation. The Bureau of Labor Statistics has extensive salary information in the Occupational Outlook Handbook, although this information does not include geographic breakdown. Please note that many sites charge for more detailed information or require a membership or subscription.

Salary Negotiation

Questions regarding compensation are some of the most uncomfortable questions for job applicants. Often, applicants do not know how to effectively ask or answer questions about salary. Effective salary negotiation involves research, confidence, timing, and salesmanship.

The first universal point to understand about salary is that employers pay for the position, not the person. The position has a wage range, and anyone occupying that position will earn in that range. No, this is not entirely fair, but is the way it is. Everyone wants more money: the applicant, the employees, and the employers.

This leads to a second point: If you focus strictly on how much you will be paid, you may be perceived as a mercenary, someone who only wants to do the job, get paid, and go home. If you are looking for career growth, longevity with an employer, and growth within the organization, then salary questions need to be handled tactfully.

To illustrate this point, let's look at an example. A candidate for an hourly kitchen position would like $.05 more per hour than what is being offered. We will assume that the employer is observing all employment laws.

> $.05 per hour x 8-hour shift = $.40 per day
> $.40 x 5-day workweek = $2.00 per week

Let's also assume that this position entails not 40 hours per week, but 50, so that is 10 hours of overtime at time-and-a-half:

> $.05 x 1.5 = $.075 x 10 hours = $.75

This equals a weekly total of $2.75.

> $2.75 x 52 weeks = $143.00 per year benefit to the
> employee, before taxes

The employer also has to consider required benefits (unemployment insurance, Social Security, and so on), which equal approximately 15 percent of an employee's salary:

> **$143.00 + 15% = $164.45 cost to the employer**

You also have to consider how that money will be made. If you assume an average of a 5 percent profit margin (which is very generous), you see:

> **$164.45 / 5% = $3,289. The employer will need to generate an additional $3,289 to maintain the same profit margin and pay the employee $.05 per hour more.**

An employer who is aware of their numbers will know this and will be able to find someone who will work for $.05 per hour less than what the applicant is asking for. For the applicant, the challenge is to demonstrate that you are worth this investment.

In general, it is advisable not to bring up salary in an initial interview. The initial interview is best spent determining if you are right for the position and if the position is right for you. On a very basic level, negotiation can only happen if each party has something the other wants. There can really be no negotiation of salary if both parties have not yet made themselves out to be desirable commodities. There are exceptions, of course. Some advertisements and applications ask for desired salary or salary requirements from applicants in the initial stages. Some employers will ask about salary expectations during the first round of interviews.

Salary information is one of the few areas in which we do *not* suggest obtaining information from your network. It can be seen as inappropriate to ask someone in your network to divulge information about financial status. Do this research before applying for a position. This way you will be prepared if the employer asks for salary information as a part of the application process. Some employers ask about salary early as a way to reduce the number of applications that make it to the next round. Applicants who are too low or too high in their expectations are viewed as not having done their research and are dropped from consideration. You can formulate your own opinions regarding companies who screen applicants based on their desired salary, just as companies can formulate their own opinions regarding applicants who ask about salary early in the interview process.

Determining Your Value

Your research provides you with a salary range. Self-analysis allows you to make a fair determination about where you should fall within that range. Have you met or exceeded all the desired qualifications at face value? That is the best argument for starting at the upper end of the spectrum. Do you meet most of the qualifications? Then you will most likely fall in the middle of the range. Do you have a lot of potential, a great attitude, and the ability to grow quickly within the position, but lack many of the desired qualifications? You will probably start at the lower end of the spectrum.

The entire application and interview process has been about telling your potential employer what your value might be. Every employer has to decide whether the applicant is a good investment for their company. Think back to the previous math example. An increase of $.05 per hour at a 5 percent profit margin requires an additional $3,289 in sales. If the applicant does not work out after a year, in order to make back that $3,289 (which would have been saved if they had hired someone for $.05 per hour less), they have to sell an additional $65,780 ($3,289 / 5%) in product.

When you are determining your value, you should try to view the situation from the perspective of the employer, but not at the expense of your own needs. Everyone has certain financial obligations to meet, such as rent/mortgage, utility bills, groceries, transportation expenses, and student loans. Be realistic and try to differentiate the things you need from the things you want. You need to eat; it is essential. But eating out at a restaurant is a choice. You need to get to and from work, so some form of transportation is a necessity, whether it is a car or public transport. A sports car that takes ultra premium gasoline is not a necessity.

Creating a monthly budget based upon your needs will give you a clear indication of what you must net ("net" is actual take-home pay, as opposed to "gross," which is your entire salary, before taxes and deductions) each month to maintain positive financial status. **An example of a budget is:**

Housing: $_____

Utilities: $_____

Transportation: $_____

Food: $_____

Loan payment: $_____

Credit card payment: $_____

Insurance: $_____

Clothing (and laundry): $_____

Entertainment: $_____

Savings: $_____

Total Monthly Expenses: $_____
x 12

Total Annual Expenses: $_____

Based upon your research and self-analysis, you now have an objective way to determine whether or not you are able to accept a position if it is offered.

Summary

All of the effort you put into creating a résumé has paid off in the form of an interview. Interviewing takes practice and preparation. Understanding expectations, common pitfalls, what may be asked, and what to ask will make you more comfortable during this stressful occasion, giving you an advantage over other candidates. The goal of an interview is to receive an offer, but what happens after you receive an offer? How do you decide between offers? How do you negotiate salary? How do you remain positive if you do not receive an offer? Having the answers to these questions in mind can keep you at ease throughout the process.

Exercises

Exercise 1: ## Interviewing

Earlier in the chapter, we discussed the following common interview questions:

Tell me about yourself?

_____

_____

_____

What are your strengths and weaknesses?

_____

_____

_____

Why did you leave (or are you leaving) your last (or current) job?

_____

_____

_____

Tell me about a time when you had a conflict with a co-worker.

_____

_____

_____

Tell me a joke.

_____

_____

_____

Do you have any questions for me?

_____

_____

_____

Create written answers to these questions and store them in your career filing cabinet. Work with a friend or mentor, and have him or her ask you these questions. Answer without looking at your written responses. Have your helper ask you some of the other common questions found in Appendix III (see page 251), at random. Ask your friend to observe your mannerisms (eye contact, hand gestures, fidgeting) and your vocal mannerisms (such as "umm" and "like" and any other nonsense or repeated words you use). If you have the resources, record yourself (either audio only or audio-visual) so that you can hear and see how you appear when you are answering questions.

Exercise 2:

Create a Budget and Determine Your Salary Range

Using the table from earlier in the chapter, prepare a monthly budget for yourself to determine your absolute minimum required take-home salary. Utilize online resources to find a salary range for a job title that interests you. Working with a friend, negotiate the salary to your favor. Work to create a series of reasons why you should be higher on the scale. Ask your friend to challenge you. Again, if you have the resources, record (audio only or audio visual) this session. Notice how you react to repeated resistance and make adjustments if necessary.

Exercise 3:

Accepting and Declining

Create two professional letters, one accepting an offer and one declining an offer. With the acceptance letter, work to demonstrate enthusiasm for the position while confirming details such as start date, salary, and benefits package. With the declination letter, work on remaining positive and creating a lasting connection—you may reapply to that employer in the future.

five

THE NOVICE CULINARIAN: EDUCATION AND EXPERIENCE

ONE OF THE MORE COMMON IMAGES used to describe career progression is that of a path. The idea is that there is a starting point, perhaps a desired end point or perhaps not, and one progresses along this path throughout one's career. The path has many intersections and can be circuitous, and there are times when one must carve a way through the landscape rather than following a previously designed path.

We would like to offer a different image, one of a career tree. We like this image because a tree continually grows upward and outward and it draws from, is a part of, and interacts with its environment. Your career is living, constantly evolving, and three-dimensional. A small seed of interest, when given the correct environment and nutrients, begins to sprout. The roots are your interests and influences, which continually feed the entire system.

The trunk is your foundation — your education and training — which provides the support. As you continue to learn, the foundation becomes broader. From your foundation, you begin to branch out, often in multiple directions, over the course of time. As you continue to progress, refine, and specialize, the branches continue to sprout. Your individual tree is in a forest, and the branches of one begin to intermingle with those of another. The individuals become part of a canopy, blurring the line between, say, culinary career and education, or any number of other possibilities.

Your career tree's growth will progress through three stages, which are roughly equivalent to levels of the craft guild system of old. In the early stages of your career, you are a novice, or an apprentice, learning the craft through on-the-job training and/or formal education. Having gained proficiency, you become ready to move into the next stage, that of the "journeyman." In modern terms, this is a point where you are taking on supervisory roles, assuming responsibility for others rather than being accountable for your own production. After many years and much work you progress to the next stage, that of "master." We are not suggesting that you will know everything there is to know about your craft; this is the stage where you are assuming the highest amount of responsibility. This is also the stage where you share your extensive knowledge with others through coaching, mentoring, and teaching.

Every individual's growth will be different. Some may reach a high level in one aspect of their career and decide to pursue another avenue, in effect going from master to novice. As you progress, continue to make new goals and reflect upon the goals you have made so that you are continually moving yourself forward.

The Novice

Now it is time to create a foundation and build toward your career. At this point, you should have the building blocks for a résumé from your filing cabinet, a network of connections, and a map of your career goals. These

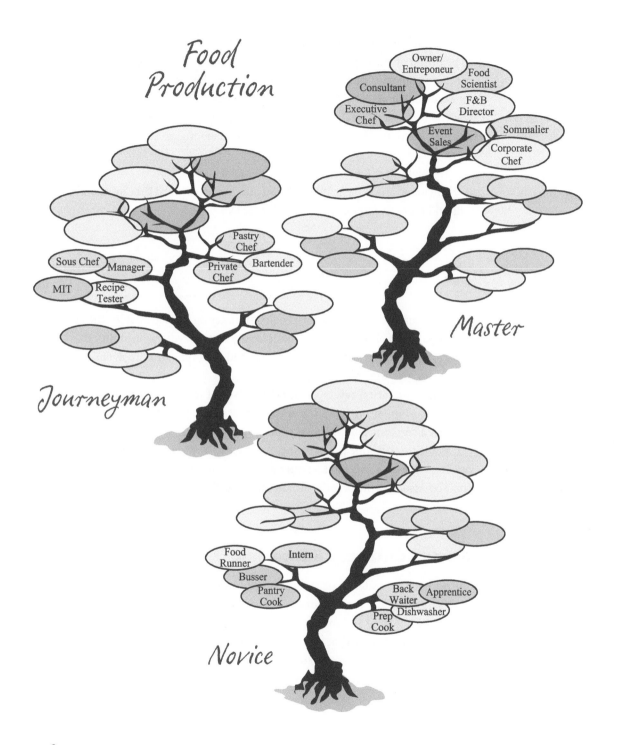

Food Production

Owner/
Entreponeur

Food
Scientist

Consultant

F&B
Director

Executive
Chef

Event
Sales

Sommalier

Corporate
Chef

Master

Pastry
Chef

Sous Chef   Manager

Private
Chef

Bartender

MIT   Recipe
Tester

Journeyman

Food
Runner

Intern

Busser

Back
Waiter

Apprentice

Pantry
Cook

Prep
Cook

Dishwasher

Novice

Career trees

may not be very extensive, since you are early in your career. It is important to be proud of the experience and education you do have and to be able to communicate your potential to prospective employers rather than focusing on a lack of experience. You have to begin where you are, not from where you wish you were. Realize as well that almost no one in any industry begins a career at a pinnacle point. It takes years of learning, growth, and development to climb the career tree.

The right first job for your career depends upon a number of factors. We have included some basic information about a few typical first jobs, and you will find more in Appendix II (see page 241).

Education

There are many different types of educational programs available. The type of program you choose depends upon many factors: your age, ability to access programs, cost, type of degree offered, and type of school, college, or university offering the program.

Your foundation can be created by means of formal education, formal apprenticeship, or on-the-job training; most likely, your foundation will be built on a combination of these items.

Achieving an educational benchmark early in your career may be more practical than attempting to return to school later when there are more complex issues (work, family, finances, and so forth) making demands on your time.

Formal Culinary Education

The decision to undertake formal culinary education is not one to take lightly. As with any formal education, you must weigh the value of your investment of time and money and the quality of the program against the return on investment that you will see over the course of your career. Education does allow you the opportunity to gain an understanding of and to practice basic skills that you can then apply throughout your career.

A culinary classroom

While on-the-job training may teach you one way to do something and how to do it well in a particular environment, formal education provides you with the method and the reasons behind the method, which will allow you to adapt to a variety of circumstances. Ultimately, formal education alone will not guarantee you any specific job, nor will it provide you with all of the skills you could ever possibly need; it provides a base of knowledge that will build as your experience builds.

The true value of formal education is easiest to judge in terms of the career path you would like to undertake. Use your goals from chapter 2, and search the job titles on job boards. Read the desired qualifications. If you repeatedly see a certain degree or level of education as a requirement, then you will need that degree even to be added to the pile of potential candidates, let alone to make it through to the interview stage.

Some long-term goals may require a combination of educational experiences. For instance, a restaurant manager may need formal culinary training and formal business education, while a food writer may need a journalism or writing degree in addition to culinary education.

Vocational Training Programs

Some high schools have culinary vocational training programs. If you are in high school, are considering a culinary career, and this option is available to you, it is a wise choice to consider to gain an introduction to the industry while learning a base of hands-on skills.

Certificate Programs

Certificate programs are available for professionals and food enthusiasts. These programs tend to be focused in subject and short in duration. They may be a combination of lectures and knowledge sharing and hands-on production, and they are offered through colleges, universities, community centers, and professional organizations. At the end of the program, you receive a certificate of attendance and perhaps continuing education credits. These programs can introduce a new field or area, offer additional education to increase your current knowledge base, and provide an opportunity to network.

Continuing Education

Continuing education (CE) classes are generally very short in length and focus on a specific subject. Some courses may award CE credits and a certificate of completion. CE classes are a great way to bolster your knowledge in a specific area. If you are considering a culinary school that offers continuing education classes, taking a class before applying to that school will provide unique insight into the program, instructors, campus, and teaching style.

Earning a bachelor's degree

Associate Degree

An associate degree is awarded after the completion of a two-year program at an accredited institution. There are several types of associate degrees, such as Associate in Arts (AA), Associate in Science (AS), Associate in Applied Science (AAS), and Associate in Occupational Studies (AOS), with a variety of majors. The AA degree requires a higher percentage of liberal arts requirements, and the AOS requires fewer liberal arts courses than the AA does. The AAS and AOS degrees are geared toward those who intend to enter the workforce upon graduation. In terms of culinary and baking and pastry programs, AAS and AOS degrees are primarily hands-on degrees; the programs teach specific skills of the trade that are immediately and directly usable upon graduation.

Bachelor's Degree

A bachelor's degree usually requires four years of full-time study to complete. Some students begin by earning an associate degree and then transferring to a bachelor's program, and others enter a bachelor's program directly. As with associate degrees, there are several types of bachelor's degrees based upon the number of liberal arts courses required. Some common degrees are: Bachelor of Arts (at least half of the course work is in liberal arts), Bachelor of Science (approximately half of the course work is in liberal arts), Bachelor of Professional Studies, and Bachelor of Fine Arts (around one-quarter of the course work is in liberal arts).

Possession of a bachelor's degree is often a requirement for higher-level positions (management and above). Some fields may require specific degrees, such as a BS in business for a management position or a BA in journalism or writing for an editorial position, whereas others require the degree but are not specific about the major. Some majors that culinary professionals commonly pursue are: culinary arts/baking and pastry arts management, business administration, hospitality and tourism management, and hotel administration. Those considering specific career paths, such as research and development, viniculture, or communications, would be wise to pursue degrees in those majors.

Master's Degree

Master's degrees are for those who wish to demonstrate a high level of knowledge in a particular field. Since many who pursue master's degrees are working professionals taking classes part-time while they continue to work, most universities allow five to seven years for the completion of the degree. To be eligible to pursue a master's degree, one must possess a bachelor's degree. Depending upon the major, some programs may require specific undergraduate course work in addition to a bachelor's degree, such as statistics for a business degree; or chemistry, biology, and anatomy for a nutritional sciences degree. Individuals may pursue a master's degree immediately upon completion of a bachelor's degree; however, many first gain experience in their chosen field before pursuing this level of degree.

Some professions, such as those involving science, require master's-level degrees or higher as a matter of course, whereas others, such as management, look favorably upon master's degrees for executive-level positions.

Doctorates

Doctoral degrees are the highest level of education. These degrees are commonly pursued by those who are interested in teaching at a college level and those involved in scientific research. Those completing doctoral degrees possess an extremely advanced knowledge base and mastery in their chosen field. As a capstone project, most doctoral degrees require the production of a book-length, publishable work that is defended against a panel of instructors.

What to Look for in a Culinary School

The value of a college degree lies in its accreditation, and more specifically, in the quality of the accrediting body. The United States Department of Education (USDE) states: "The goal of accreditation is to ensure that education provided by institutions of higher education meets acceptable levels of quality. Accrediting agencies, which are private educational associations of regional or national scope, develop evaluation criteria and conduct peer evaluations to assess whether or not those criteria are met. Institutions

Look for a varied curriculum

and/or programs that request an agency's evaluation and that meet an agency's criteria are then 'accredited' by that agency;" and "The U.S. Department of Education does not accredit educational institutions and/or programs. However, the Secretary of Education is required by law to publish a list of nationally recognized accrediting agencies that the Secretary determines to be reliable authorities as to the quality of education or training provided by the institutions of higher education and the higher education programs they accredit." A list of accrediting bodies that are recognized by the USDE is available on their Web site.

The Council for Higher Education Accreditation (CHEA) maintains a database of colleges and universities that have been accredited by entities that are reviewed for quality by either the CHEA or the USDE. This database is accessible by visiting the CHEA's Web site.

Accreditation makes the degree program worth the time and money you are investing. This is important for several reasons. A college or university must be accredited in order to be eligible for federal financial aid. At The Culinary Institute of America, for example, approximately 90 percent of our students receive some form of financial aid, making accreditation vital to ensure both the quality of education and the ability of students to afford that education.

In the longer term, employers may not honor a degree from a nonaccredited institution (or one accredited by a nonrecognized entity), eliminating you from contention for a job. Furthermore, if you look to obtain the next level of education from a particular institution, that institution will not recognize your previous degree if it is from a nonaccredited institution.

Evaluating a Culinary Curriculum

Following accreditation, curriculum, which is the actual course of study, is the next most important consideration.

If you are going to invest in formal education, commit to visiting the college before making any decisions. Take a formal tour. Notice the facilities. Are the kitchens and classrooms clean and in good repair? Is the equipment modern — both in the kitchens and in the lecture classrooms?

If the school has a public restaurant, take the opportunity to eat there to experience firsthand the quality of food they are producing. Speak with students (other than those conducting the tour) about their experiences, about what they like and do not like, and whether they would recommend the program. Are the students and faculty polite? Are they professional in appearance and dress? After all, this is the hospitality industry, so it is reasonable to expect that the school require its employees and students to embody the spirit of hospitality.

Visiting Schools

Learning to cook and bake requires a hands-on, experiential learning environment in addition to book work and study. **Some important considerations for any cooking or baking program include the following:**

○ *Compare how much time is spent in hands-on kitchen laboratories.*

○ *Review and compare the progression of the classes. It is most beneficial to build a base knowledge of cuisine, product and equipment identification, and techniques before attempting to learn specialties.*

○ *Compare applied work experience requirements — called either an "internship" or "externship" — where you have the opportunity to demonstrate and hone the skills you have learned in a real-world production kitchen.*

○ *Compare the student-to-teacher ratios and class sizes of various schools. This offers insight as to how much individual attention you are able to receive as you learn.*

In addition to developing the skills to cook and bake well, success in the hospitality industry also requires soft skills, such as the ability to communicate effectively both verbally and in writing, business sense, an understanding of the history and modern relevancy of the industry, and human resource skills. Identify that writing, math, communication, history, and business management courses are a part of that school's program.

A solid program needs quality instructors. Look for instructor biographies on the school's Web site. Notice the instructors' professional certifications, their length of time in the industry, and their progression through the industry. Notice as well their educational backgrounds. Seasoned and experienced alumni returning to teach is a positive reflection on the college.

The college experience is about more than just classroom time. Strong support services, including a well-stocked library, academic advising, counseling, tutoring, information technology, financial aid, and career services departments will contribute to your experience and afford you the opportunity for academic and career success. On-campus clubs, organizations, recreational facilities, and events will contribute to your social and emotional success.

The Applied Work Experience

One of the most intense learning experiences of culinary school is the applied work experience, also known as an internship or externship. In some programs, the internship occurs within the program, while with others, it occurs as a capstone at the end of the program.

Some schools place students in their internships, meaning that the school makes the connection and arrangements for the student, whereas others place the responsibility on the student so that the process of pros-

Finding the applied work experience

*T*he reasons for selecting an internship location will be different for everyone. Your internship choices may be prescribed by the nature of the course in which you are enrolled. A culinary program will most likely require an internship stressing hands-on production, for instance. This means that even if your goal is to get a position in management, your internship will still stress practical culinary and kitchen skills. Regardless of your ultimate goal, approach this job search as you would any future job search.

○ Start early. Allow yourself the time to work through the process. Your career is your responsibility.

○ Use your long-term and intermediate career goals to determine the types of experiences that will be most beneficial to you.

○ Talk with your career services advisors, academic advisor, mentor, and instructors. Make an appointment and bring your goals. They will have recommendations for you. Even if they do not tell you where to go, they can offer possibilities.

○ Research these possibilities. Find other students who have gone to these locations and talk to them about their experiences. Research the location and the team as you would for a job search.

○ Research collateral elements. How are you going to get to the location? Where will you live? How will you get to and from work? How will you pay for groceries, gas, bills? The budget worksheet in the Salary Negotiation section of chapter 4 is another useful tool.

○ Make a list to compare your goals and desired outcomes versus each possibility. Record your research in one place (one spreadsheet, one piece of paper, or one chart) so that you can view all the possibilities side by side. Rate the possibilities. This is very similar to how you will evaluate multiple job offers in the future.

○ Apply to all of your possibilities. A common worry among students is that they feel they have no chance with their top choices because they do not have much experience. It is true that there can be a lot of competition; however, if you do not apply for what you want, you have absolutely no chance of securing that position. Internship employers understand that this is a foundational experience. Present yourself well, focus on what you can contribute, and be persistent. Utilize the tips on applying, following up, and interviewing in chapters 3 and 4 to prepare yourself for this "mini" version of a job search.

○ Remember that an internship is a class. There may be certain restrictions and requirements that students and employers must meet in order to complete this class successfully. Remember that if a situation does not work for your internship, the possibilities are still endless after graduation. "No" for an internship does not mean "no" forever. Focus your energy on successfully completing the class so that you can successfully complete your degree. Then you are free to pursue your goals.

pecting, applying for, and securing the position becomes a skill set that is learned during the course of study. Very rarely in your career will anyone just hand you a job. The process of securing your internship, even if frustrating, mirrors the challenges you will face during the job search. Take this opportunity to build job-searching skills now so that you can use them effectively upon graduation.

Consider this as you research culinary schools. The more work and responsibility you, as a student, must take on to secure your internship, the better off you will be in the long run.

An internship is an agreement and a mutually beneficial relationship between the school, the student, and the employer. The school agrees to grant a set number of educational credits upon the successful completion of the internship. The employer agrees to host the student and provide training. The student agrees to work to the standards of the employer and complete any course work (most often a portfolio or written summary of the experience) required by the school.

The school has the expectation that the student will be a positive representative of the school and behave in accordance with school policies. It also anticipates that the employer will provide training appropriate to the student's course of study. There are additional expectations: that the employer will maintain a positive and safe environment for the student and complete any required ratings or feedback forms that document and evaluate the student's experience.

The student expects that the employer will provide a working, educational environment where he or she can increase skills, ask questions, and even make mistakes in a positive environment, and that the school will be available to guide, coach, and mentor the student through the positive and challenging aspects of the experience.

The employer expects the students to act according to the standards the company has set for that position (for example, if that position works sixty-plus hours per week, then that is what the student will be expected to work); that the students will produce quality work according to their abilities and the standards of the employer; and that they will demonstrate growth over the course of their time with the employer. The employer expects that the school will prepare students adequately for the type of work they will perform and that the school will remain available to coach and mentor the students through all aspects of the internship, whether positive or negative.

- Be an observer. An internship is a foundational experience; students are hired to learn how the business operates. They are expected to contribute to the best of their ability. Often, the way that particular business runs may be different from the ways you learned in school or the ways you have seen in the past. Keep an open mind and learn what they do, how they do it, and perhaps why they do it that way. Techniques and methods that may seem contrary to your beliefs are still valid. You grow as a culinarian by respecting and incorporating the immense diversity in this industry. When the experience is over, you can decide if you want to follow the techniques and methods of that one employer or not.

- Take the time to get to know everyone. Your supervisor will be a valuable and expected reference. Your coworkers will move around and up, so they may be hiring by the time you graduate.

- Look for opportunities to learn. The education of an internship is not the same as the education at school. There will most likely not be lectures, demos, or detailed explanations as a matter of course. The primary goal is to ensure service to the guest.

- Doing routine tasks? Challenge yourself. Time yourself and work to beat your time, improving speed. Strive to work cleaner, faster, and with a more positive attitude than those around you.

- Ask for more responsibility. Come in on days off to learn other stations or aspects of the business.

- Use your time off to read and study industry publications, to network with other employers in the area, and to experiment on your own. There is always something to learn, and your education is your responsibility.

Although many students are offered positions with the employer when they graduate, this is not required, nor should there be an expectation that an offer will be given or accepted.

Frequently Asked Questions about the Applied Work Experience

Q How am I going to be hired without any experience?

A: *This is a very common fear, especially if students are interested in working at top properties. Employers who partner with schools realize that students go on internships to increase their skill level. They are not hiring, nor are they expecting students to run their business. They are looking for students who* *are eager and willing to learn. Demonstrate these traits in your application materials. Employers expect that students will leave the internship with much more skill than when they arrived. At The Culinary Institute of America, with each returning group of externs, we ask, by a show of hands, how many students were offered a position to continue with their extern employer following graduation? About 75 percent of the members of every group has received an offer. That is a testament to the great work, the amount of learning, and the ability to adapt that students display on their externship. Know that you will be able to deliver as well.*

Q I want to be a food writer (or recipe tester or food stylist). Should I do my internship at a magazine or in a traditional kitchen?

A: *There are many options for specialization within the culinary field, but remember, at the core of any culinary career is the basic knowledge of how to cook in a professional environment. At some point, you should plan to practice the craft of professional cooking. Not only will being able to execute culinary skills in the real world give you credence (how can you accurately develop, communicate, and style food if you have not first practiced the craft of producing food for an audience?), it provides you with a useful, practical job skill. Many writers, recipe testers, and stylists work part-time freelance initially and, in time, the side job becomes the main job. Being able to earn a living allows you to work toward your long-term goals. Internships in publishing are notoriously unpaid. For some it is more practical to take on a temporary, unpaid experience while still a student, and then build professional cooking experience following graduation. Regardless of whether you decide to pursue an internship at a magazine or not, you can (and should) practice writing every day, read every day, and network with writers, editors, recipe testers, and stylists at every opportunity.*

Q Should I take a paid or unpaid internship?

A: *An internship is an educational experience, not a moneymaking venture. Carefully consider both short- and long-term goals when deciding upon this experience. Identify how working for a given employer will advance your career (long-term goals). In the short term, you will need to have a place to live, feed yourself, get to and from work, wash your clothes, and pay your bills. All of these things require money. Plan for these costs. An unpaid intern may not be eligible to receive workers' compensation in the event of an on-the-job injury. In an industry where you are around sharp, hot, slippery, and heavy items and often operate in a state of fatigue, this is a very important element to consider. Having health insurance is highly recommended. Prepare yourself mentally: The payoff of an internship is the experience. Make sure you have a plan to take an active part in your own learning.*

Q Should I go overseas for my internship?

A: *Immersing yourself in another culture is an invaluable learning experience, but traveling and working internationally requires much more planning than obtaining an experience domestically.*

○ *You will need a passport.*

○ *You will need to be able to communicate in the language of the country. Your application materials (résumé and e-mail correspondences) will most likely need to be in that language. Even if the kitchen speaks your language, you will still need to locate housing, get to and from the airport, get to and from work, go to the market, and so on, which will all require interacting with native speakers.*

○ *In order to work legally you will need the appropriate visa. Every country has specific visa types and requirements. Research these on the consulate's Web site of individual countries. Some common requirements, in addition to the application, are: passport, offer of employment, proof of student status, proof of insurance, round-trip plane ticket (yes, purchased before applying for the visa), and financial statements. Often you will need to go, in person, to the consulate office nearest to your permanent residence.*

○ *Consider the world's economic climate. Opportunities for internships in other countries may be limited in a down economy — there is a responsibility to employ citizens first.*

Q I do not want to do grunt work on my internship.

A: *Not a question, but it's a common comment. Internships are designed to build upon skills learned in school. Everyone should expect to start at an entry level on his or her internship. Demonstrate your culinary skills and your ability to follow directions, and you may advance on merit. Displaying the attitude* *that any task is beneath you will guarantee one of two things — that you will be doing that task for your entire time, or you will be terminated from the experience. Eventually you will be a leader, and you will need to motivate others to do those tasks. Every task is an important part of serving the guest. Keep this clear, and you will be able to motivate others; forget this, and you will have a staff that cuts corners and grumbles their way through the shift.*

Apprenticeship

The American Culinary Federation (ACF) operates and administers a formal apprenticeship program for young culinarians. An apprenticeship is a structured, hands-on, learn-as-you-work education.

The ACF offers two- and three-year programs requiring 4,000 and 6,000 work hours, respectively, at an approved facility and 576 classroom hours in twelve mandatory courses. To learn more about ACF apprenticeships, search for "American Culinary Federation," and click on "Certify," "Apprentice," and "Become an Apprentice."

Getting a Degree from the School of Hard Knocks

The hospitality industry is very fortunate to be an industry in which individuals can grow and advance through on-the-job training alone. This is a very challenging method of education. There is a length of time involved, usually spanning several different jobs or employers, to learn skills and techniques.

You will need to study yourself, create reading lists, research information, and more. Unlike schools where you might be able to ask your teachers about the hows and whys of a particular technique, you may need to find the answers on your own. There is the added pressure of immediate need for performance; when you are working, the goal is to get the work done as quickly and efficiently to standard as possible, not necessarily to understand the whys and wider applications for the work that you are doing. Formal education condenses and streamlines this process, providing a base and a resource for your future growth.

The Self-Taught Culinarian

During the term of the apprenticeship, the apprentice works in one facility under the guidance of an ACF-certified (or certification-eligible) executive chef. In addition to work and classroom experiences, the apprentice is involved with their ACF chapter and is expected to participate in events and competitions. At the conclusion of the apprenticeship period, the apprentice is eligible to test to become a Certified Culinarian or Certified Pastry Culinarian, or Certified Sous Chef or Certified Working Pastry Chef.

Informal Education: On-the-Job Training

According to Bureau of Labor Statistics information, culinary careers up through supervisory and management positions are learned primarily through on-the-job training and promotion. It is true that experience is the top selling point; an employer knows you can do the job because you have done a similar job.

Planning your own education through work experience alone takes a very dedicated mindset, especially as you create a foundation and at those points when you are looking to build skills to climb to the next level.

The actual physical coordination and execution of tasks are learned through practice and repetition — you are shown the way a task is done, and you repeat it. This will happen as you begin any job. The challenge for someone who is self-educating is to learn why that task is done in that way so that you can identify other methods that yield the same result (even if they are not used at that location), react and recover if something goes wrong, and broaden the application to other uses. These discoveries require research on your own and the ability to identify reliable and knowledgeable sources so that you can ask questions and increase your knowledge. On-the-job training is a part of everyone's education — culinary skills are learned and refined through practice and application. Successful culinarians need to be self-motivated to ask questions; experiment to refine techniques; and read, research, and network outside of work hours.

Entry-Level Work Experience

Whether you are new to the workforce or new to the hospitality industry, it is beneficial to gain some foundational experience before fully immersing yourself into gaining an education and creating a culinary career tree. As a novice, someone with no to little skill in a professional environment, this means starting in an entry-level position.

Entry level is just that, a beginning. Examples of these positions include dishwasher, prep cook, busser, food runner, bar back, host/hostess, quick-service counter or production, retail clerk, and tasting room assistant. These positions do not require a great deal of specialized skills to obtain the job (although they all have specific skills needed to do the job well), so they are accessible to novices. Because of this, they are at the lower end of the pay scale and may involve more repetitive work than those positions higher up the ladder.

These experiences lay the foundation for higher learning. They require that you show up on time, in uniform, and perform tasks as directed quickly and repeatedly. Instilling this discipline early in your career leads to success later. Your limits may be challenged; completing a twelve-hour day in the heat and stress of a busy kitchen for the first time is exhausting. The greatest challenge may be going back the next day — and the next, and the day after that. In this way, you build up endurance, confidence, and fortitude.

At The Culinary Institute of America, as a prerequisite for admission, we require a minimum of six months of experience in an operation that produces 80 percent of its product in house. Although not a long time when compared with the length of a career, six months is enough time to determine if pursuing further education, an apprenticeship, or further on-the-job training is right for you.

Gaining Entry-Level Experience

Your culinary career, regardless of where it may end up, needs to be built upon a solid foundation. In cooking, stock is referred to as *fond*. It is the base. Without a good stock, you will never create a good sauce. Without quality ingredients, you cannot create a quality product.

The foundation of a culinary career is hands-on production. Even if you do not envision yourself spending much of your career in production, having a

An obstacle that many face early on (and at times, not so early on) is that they feel that they are doing menial work — jobs that no one else wants to do. Entry-level jobs are difficult, tedious, and do not pay well; it is understandable to want to have the opportunity to move up and not do the "dirty work." It is essential to your career to overcome this mindset early. Every aspect of every job in the hospitality industry is important because in some way it touches our guests. The most successful people adopt the attitude that everything matters. On a very practical level, entry-level positions keep our industry strong.

Remember that everything you do is ultimately for the guest, whether you are peeling onions or sweeping the floor. When your guests are happy, they will create more business either by returning or by telling others about their positive experience. The more business there is, the greater the opportunities for you. Remember as well that if your goal is to progress to a higher position, you will need to be able to demonstrate and inspire those below you to do their jobs well.

solid, practical understanding of ingredients, techniques, and applications will allow you to do your job better. It is very difficult to describe or communicate about something in which you have no practical experience, and having done the job provides you with the ability to understand, motivate, and streamline work others are doing.

At this early point in your career, you may not have anything in your résumé filing cabinet, and you may not have many network connections (or, if coming from another industry, you may not have any résumé items or connections that can be of great assistance with your culinary career). This is okay at this stage of the game. Dress neatly (no one is expecting suits when applying for entry-level culinary positions) and go to restaurants, diners, quick-service establishments, cafés, and pizza places and fill out applications. No calls, no e-mails, but show up ready to interview and ready to work if needed. Your desire to work hard is your selling point, and you demonstrate that by showing up in person. Practice telling the managers that you are a hard worker, will show up on time, and will do what you are told.

Maximizing the Experience

If you are taking a job to have a job, you can just show up to work every day, perform your tasks, and go home. **If you are taking a job because you are looking to gain experience and insight into a possible career path, keep the following points in mind:**

- **Observe.** *Learn what you need to do, do it well, and watch what others are doing. Watch the work flow, the organization. You will begin to see who the superstars are very quickly. Watch both what they do and how they do it. Copy their actions.*

- **Record.** *Write things down, from tasks, prep lists, and techniques to the names of your co-workers, owners, supervisors, delivery drivers, sales people, and VIP guests. Keep a small notebook in your pocket, and then transcribe this information and transfer it into your filing cabinet.*

- **Listen.** *Listen to what people say and how they say it. It is very difficult to learn anything when talking or waiting to talk.*

- **Help out other people.** *Show up early and stay until everyone is caught up. Offer your assistance when you have the time. People are more inclined to help you out if they know you will return the favor.*

- **Admit your mistakes and learn from them.** *You will screw up, sometimes quite badly. You will incur wrath. Learn what happened (ask at a later time if necessary, when things have cooled down), and try not to let the same thing happen again.*

- **Ask for help.** *It can be hard to admit that you need help. Just remember that the guests do not care about your pride; they only care that what they ordered comes to the table accurately and in a reasonable amount of time.*

- **Show up on time (early), in uniform, as scheduled for every shift.** *This instills discipline, pride, and respect for your co-workers, employer, and guests.*

○ **Create other opportunities to learn.** *Utilize your time off to stage (working a shift, usually without pay, to gain experience) at other establishments. Volunteer at events or food banks. Attend demonstrations, shows, and conferences.*

Joining Organizations

Become involved in your section of the industry by joining professional organizations. Attend local chapter meetings to meet other professionals in your area. Attend regional or national conferences. Ask your employer if they will cover some of the cost, as this is professional development. Hand out your business cards, collect cards from others, and send LinkedIn connection requests at every opportunity.

Become a thought leader by publishing articles, speaking at conferences, writing/guest writing/commenting on blogs, creating video content on YouTube, and so on. Take every available opportunity to expand your sphere of influence and share your knowledge and experience for the benefit of others. Doing so increases your value, gives you some leverage with your current employer, and may catch the eye of future employers.

The Importance of a Strong Network

No one acts in isolation in his or her career. You work with and for people. You have relationships with clients, customers, and guests. You create impressions upon those you meet. You can take advantage of all these connections. Networking is the purposeful and systematic creation of connections with the goal of furthering your career. Networking is not asking for a job, but rather it is about information sharing and promoting. Whenever you establish a good contact, be sure to record not only that person's contact information, but also details that will help you maintain a relationship. Jot down the notes from your meeting (the place, the occasion, others that were present, the person who introduced you, what you talked about, the next steps that were mentioned, the introduction that was promised, and so on) and keep them as part of your files.

Identifying Your Existing Network

You already have a network made up of family, friends, current and former co-workers, and casual acquaintances. In chapter 2, you created some short-term, intermediate, and long-term goals. Reviewing your goals, can you think of anyone you know who already occupies any of the jobs or possesses any of the knowledge you are looking to obtain? Is there anyone you know who has a similar position or is involved in the same industry you are looking to pursue? Create a list of any names that come to mind.

From this list, match the names to your goals to help you to identify why you would want to speak with that particular person. If you are currently looking for a job or a better opportunity, it is in your best interest to speak with people whose sphere of influence works most directly with your short-term goal of becoming employed. Having identified someone who holds a job similar to one of your long-term goals, you will be preparing a different set of questions.

Finding People You Do Not Know

Identifying people whom you would like to connect with that you do not currently know is a bit less direct. Again, begin with your goals. Pull out some key phrases, like job titles, names of employers you would like to work for, and levels of education or certifications you are looking to achieve. Decide what you would like to know; for instance, do you need a job now, are you looking for the next step, or are you looking to connect with someone to learn about how that individual got to where he or she is now? Begin asking your immediate connections: "I am looking to obtain this information, and by any chance do you know of someone who could help?" Ask individuals. Add this to your Facebook status or tweet it. Do something that lets others know you are looking to make a connection.

A professional networking site such as LinkedIn is a valuable tool to grow your network. The purpose of this site is to create professional, not social, connections, and it has immense search capabilities. This site allows you to search for individuals by name, company (current or past), school, location, job title, and keyword. The site allows you to connect directly to people within three degrees of separation, or to members of a shared group. The more you grow, the more you can take advantage of the site.

Pay attention to media (both the popular or general media and special interest media geared toward professionals) to identify prominent individuals in the segment of the industry where your interests lie. Who is being covered? Who is creating trends? Who is doing the things that interest you? It is very easy to use the Web to find a business address and phone for someone, so that you can gain a point of contact for a person you do not yet know.

Before You Reach Out

Before reaching out to either an existing connection or a potential new connection, it is essential to determine what you are looking to gain from this point of contact. Each point of contact should have a specific purpose, whether you are looking to satisfy an immediate need, create an ongoing relationship, or both. **Reasons to connect with someone may include the following:**

o   *Information, reference, or referral for a job.*

o   *Information regarding a particular career path.*

o   *Information regarding a particular company.*

o   *Seeking an introduction to a third party.*

o   *Sharing information within a group of peers.*

o   *Promotion of a product or service.*

Reaching Out

Having determined the person to contact and the reason(s) for connecting with him or her, plan your approach. This is quite similar to researching employers prior to applying for a job. Find out what you can about this person. If this is someone you do not know, do you have anything in common that could help break the ice and create an initial connection? Do you have a friend or connection who could introduce you or whose name you can reference when you reach out? If this is a current connection, review your past encounters with this person — when they occurred and the subject matter.

Methods for connecting vary widely according to your current relationship with that person and the purpose for connecting. In general, if you would like to speak with someone either in person or over the phone and you do not have a very close, ongoing relationship (family member, close friend, or close peer), it is wise to connect via e-mail requesting an appointment. Cold calls, unexpectedly calling, or arriving in person can create a bit of a barrier, especially if this is the first time you are connecting to someone. Cold-calling puts that person on the spot, forcing him or her to pay attention to you right now regardless of other current commitments. Many immediately associate this type of behavior with salespeople and as a result become defensive or suspicious when encountering this type of situation. An e-mail request allows the recipient time to process what you are asking and to assess their availability to create the time to answer.

When connecting with someone you do not know, begin by introducing yourself and state the reason you are connecting with him or her. Reference a common connection, if you have one, and say a little about yourself. This is similar to a cover letter; however, this will be a bit more personal — you are looking to create a personal relationship, not an employer-employee relationship. State your desired next point of contact (respond by e-mail, set up a time to speak), and close by thanking the person for his or her time and assistance. Save a copy of this correspondence in your networking file.

The following is an example of an e-mail sent to a person who is not a current connection.

To:	cruben@gooseisland.com
Cc:	
Subject:	Interested in Goose Island Brewery

Dear Mr. Ruben:

My name is Ron Hayes. I am a current student at The Culinary Institute of America. I met with Erin Decker in the Career Services Office, and she suggested I contact you. During my time at the CIA, I discovered a great interest in brewing, and pairing beer with food. I brewed my first batch with the Brew Club on campus, and am interested in learning about larger scale brewing. Could we set up a time to speak over the phone about how you went from the CIA to Goose Island Brewery, and a bit about your day-to-day responsibilities?

Thank you for your time, and I appreciate any information you are able to share. I look forward to connecting with you.

Sincerely,
Ron

Sample outreach letter

If you are connecting with a current connection, you do not need to reintroduce yourself; however, it is good to reference your past connection, especially if this is not someone with whom you have frequent exchanges:

Dear Jared:

Thank you again for speaking with me last month about your position with Goose Island....

Sample follow-up letter

Contents

As you begin to identify those currently in your network and those you wish to add to your network, create a file for each person. This can be a paper file, electronic file, Rolodex, or any other organizational tool that works for you. Your goal is to create a searchable and reviewable resource that is housed in your filing cabinet. Items to include are:

- Name, contact information, credentials/certifications, employer, and position.
- Personal information (family members, favorites, and so on).
- Common interests.
- Identifiers, if applicable (height, hair color, glasses, and so on).
- Reason for initial connection.
- Dated entries of points of contact, including date, time, subjects discussed, and plans for follow-up.

Keeping Your Network Current

You have made initial connections, and your network file has grown, but you may not need to call upon your connections for any specific information or assistance right away. The more time that passes between points of contact, the fuzzier the details may become. This makes a future connection more like an initial connection — a complete reintroduction of yourself. Maintaining regular communication with your network keeps the connections current. Your purpose with this is to provide information rather than to obtain information. The communication can be as simple as a short e-mail, or, if you are connected via LinkedIn or other network, you can post regular professional status updates. Holidays or changes in season offer a good reason to reconnect:

Dear Jared:

Happy First Day of Spring! I hope all is well in Chicago. We have lost enough snow here in New York that spring seems like a reality. I am now Vice President of the Brew Club, and at our last meeting, we tasted our hefeweizen. What new additions are you working on for the spring? Any plans for Opening Day? (Go Cubs!)

Best Wishes,
Ron

Sample follow-up letter

Mentors: A Special Kind of Network Connection

Most of your network connections can be considered casual. You may have regular exchanges with them and even call upon them for specific information from time to time, but they are not your most trusted confidants. A mentor is a specific type of network connection. This person plays an active, long-term role in your professional development. Mentors do not make decisions for you, hand you jobs or a career, or provide all the answers. Rather, they act as a coach, sounding board, and voice of reason as you move through your career. The greatest benefit to having a mentor is that the relationship forces you to reflect upon, think about, and take responsibility for your professional path.

Finding a Mentor

Establishing a relationship with a mentor can be the result of a formal program or an outgrowth of a professional relationship. Some colleges and employers offer formal mentor programs, in which an individual is paired with an alumnus, an instructor, or a senior-level employee. This relationship may be monitored by a specific office, and it often involves a formal commitment and formal check-in points. If your college or employer offers such a program, take full advantage of it!

Outside of an established program, the mentor-mentee relationship may not be so formal. One does not typically go to another and ask that person to be a mentor; it is a relationship that develops over time. A mentor generally occupies a senior position in line with your long-term goals. You may find this person as you build your network, he or she may be an instructor, or the person may work for the same employer. You should discuss your short- and long-term goals and direction with the person and ask for advice. You may also do this off and on with individuals who are not mentors. The defining points of the relationship are consistency of interactions and long-term contact.

Whether a formally organized relationship or one that has grown organically, the mentor-mentee connection is most effective and beneficial when it has some structure. Establish a regular contact pattern that works for you both. Schedule these times as a meeting on both of your calendars, creating accountability for both parties. Come to the meeting, which can be face to face, by phone, or by video, with these items:

○ *Goals, both short and long term, and your current action plans for them.*

○ *A professional update. What is your current position? What have you learned? What are your strengths, and what do you need to work on?*

○ *An update with any follow-up from the previous meeting.*

○ *A current résumé.*

○ *A list of network connections you hope to develop (specific individuals, jobs, or companies).*

○ *Conversation topics and questions. Pick this person's brain at every opportunity.*

As with every meeting, make notes, identify items to follow up on, and send a brief thank-you note showing appreciation for your mentor's time.

Summary

In this chapter, we have presented the image of your career as a tree, a living being that develops and evolves over time. The tree's growth can be grouped into three stages: the novice, when you are learning your craft; the journeyman, when you are leading others and assuming wider responsibilities; and the master, a stage of expertise when you are directing and educating others. Here we focused on the first stage, the novice, presenting ways to utilize the education and experience gained in the early stage of your career to set yourself up for future growth. We reviewed the educational opportunities available for an aspiring culinary professional and presented examples of novice job titles taken from actual job boards. This is by no means meant to be an exhaustive list of novice culinary career possibilities; rather, it provides an overview of the skill sets and experience that employers desire at this stage of your career.

Exercises

Exercise 1: ## Continue to Build Your Career Filing Cabinet

Keep a small notebook with you at all times during your workday. Make a note every time you meet someone new (name, title, company, contact info, if available, and a couple of info bytes about this person); learn a new recipe/task/skill/technique; contribute (a daily special, referring a friend to be employed, and so on); volunteer; or learn more about the business (purveyors, for example). Schedule a weekly "career check-in" when you will take half an hour to transcribe the items from your notebook into the appropriate files in your cabinet.

Exercise 2: ## Setting the Stage for the Next Step

As your career grows, you will have to convince a potential employer to take a chance and hire you for a position for which you do not have any direct experience. This takes practice. Research next-level (supervisory) positions. These can be within your current organization or at a different employer. Find job postings and, using the information in your filing cabinet, create a résumé, cover letter, and answers to the interview questions from chapter 4 promoting yourself for this next level of position. Even though you will not have the direct experience for this position, present yourself as a valuable candidate.

six

THE JOURNEYMAN

EARLIER IN THIS BOOK, we addressed the tools and mise en place used throughout your career. The specifics of using job-search tools and tactics may change as you progress in your career (for instance, the content and format of your résumé may change significantly); however, the concepts remain valid and applicable throughout your entire career. You keep your knives sharp, even if you do not use all of them every day, so they are ready when needed. You keep your shoes shined, even if no one will see them when you are behind the stove, because at any minute a guest may want to speak with you. You keep your résumé updated, your network current, and your goals at hand because you never know when an opportunity for growth will present itself.

In the previous chapter, we took "novice" to mean the period of your career when you build a foundation and learn your craft. Regardless of where you want to end up, a culinary career is based upon the dual foundations of food and guest service. This dual foundation must be firmly rooted and understood in order to support your career tree as it widens and branches out. This foundation can only come from experience: All of the knowledge gained from education (either formally from school or from life experience) only becomes valuable to you and marketable to future employers when you put it into practice.

In this chapter, we focus on you as a "journeyman," a phase when you are able to start effecting and enacting change. At this stage in your career, you are moving up (managing people) and moving out (moving away from production or becoming a specialist). There are several skill sets at this stage that were not a focus earlier in your career, and this is a time when it is necessary and advisable to look toward additional education, such as the next level of degree or a degree more in line with your discipline, as well as toward professional certifications, as ways to further boost your future marketability.

As your knowledge, skills, and experiences increase, so do the possibilities for career growth. Some opportunities will come from the usual channels, such as job postings, internal promotion, and networking. There are also those opportunities that are not, and may never be, posted. You "create" them and then convince potential employers that the position is necessary to their success and that you are the best person for the job.

The Passive Candidate

Lucius Annaeus Seneca, a first-century Roman philosopher, said, "Luck is what happens when preparation meets opportunity." As an employee, you should not spend a large percentage of your time actively pursuing other positions. However, you should take the steps necessary to prepare yourself in case an opportunity comes your way. When you are prepared to take action on a new opportunity, even as a "passive candidate" (in other words, someone who is not actively seeking a job opportunity or career move), you are in a position to entertain such offers should they arise.

Getting Noticed Within

On the job, people watch what you do every day. You interact with subordinates, peers, associates, supervisors, and external clients in your daily quest to "get stuff done." When work is done efficiently, no one seems to notice. In truth, they should not notice — the system is supposed to operate efficiently, and workers are supposed to be proficient at their jobs. Job proficiency alone is not going to make you a desirable candidate for the next level — everyone who is considered for a position has a fairly equal skill level. When someone excels at their job every day, people begin to take notice.

People You Want to Notice You: Your Supervisor

You want your supervisor to recognize that you are doing a great job. Great reviews tend to lead to better raises. When an opportunity to advance arises, having the blessing and recommendation of your supervisor goes a long way. Review time usually comes once a year. There is a time gap between reviews, and it is easy to forget what gets accomplished between them. Take an active role in keeping your supervisor up to date with your accomplishments. Document your successes by sending short e-mail updates, "cc'ing" your supervisor on reports or intradepartmental communications, and having "stand-up" check-ins.

Demonstrate that you can identify problems and then organize and synthesize data to create and implement solutions. Do all that you can to make your boss's job easier. This is not "sucking up." This is an opportunity to gain experience, and to demonstrate and document skills at a level beyond that of your current title.

People You Want to Notice You: Your Direct Reports

Recognizing and developing the potential in your direct reports creates a positive environment. Your workers will be happy, and happy people work more efficiently. Happy workers also let others know that they have a great boss. Developing your workers is a difficult task. You have to understand their jobs, both the official job descriptions and the day-to-day circumstances and challenges they encounter as part of their job. You have to be able to identify personality types—what motivates that person, what that person responds well (and poorly) to, what he or she is very good at and what are the opportunities for growth. You have to adjust your management style to fit each individual to ensure that the whole team is running efficiently. In short, you have to listen, take notice, and care about your employees while ensuring that the business is being run within the bounds that have been set.

As you help your people to do their jobs better, there will come a time when the best opportunity for their growth is to leave your area to move up within the organization or to move up elsewhere. "Great leaders are not afraid to have great subordinates," says Richard Mignault, vice president of human resources for The Culinary Institute of America, who also has worked for more than twenty years with Hilton Hotels. When a subordinate expresses a desire to move up and out, do not be concerned about why, but rather that the person is looking to move for the right reasons. Mr. Mignault advises that your first question be "How can I help you?"

Those you help promote will also "promote" you. They will talk about the opportunities for and the environment conducive to growth that you have created. Those above you in the organization will notice that you are developing your people, demonstrating your value to the organization as a whole.

Getting Noticed Without

Companies are constantly looking for talent to improve their business. The same depth of skills and experience that makes you a desirable commodity within your current organization makes you desirable to others as well. It is easier to maintain visibility within an organization, where you are surrounded by your champions and can find potential opportunities every day. It takes a bit more effort to be visible to those outside your organization.

LinkedIn, a professional networking site, is a valuable tool because recruiters, headhunters, and search firms troll these sites in their quest to find candidates. **Take these steps to make yourself visible:**

o   *Create a public profile. LinkedIn allows you to choose the type and amounts of information you want to share. Let searchers see your name, headline, summary, specialties, current employer, and interests sections.*

o   *Use key words in your summary. Pull words from job postings and descriptions for your current level of position and the next level up. Recruiters search for candidates based upon the job description/qualifications of the position they are looking to fill.*

○ *Include an e-mail contact on your public profile so that interested parties can connect with you separately from the LinkedIn site.*

○ *Allow the Web sites category to be visible if you have a personal Web site, blog, or other items on the Web that can promote you.*

○ *Join and be active with groups. Start and comment on discussions.*

Updating Your Files

As your career advances, you need to set aside time to review your career filing cabinet. You may find that you need to add new folders, add new entries to existing folders, and weed out old items that aren't relevant any longer.

Goals

You have probably accomplished some of your short-term goals. It is a good time to look at your intermediate goals and rewrite them as short-term goals. Take the time to get specific about the tasks you need to accomplish as part of meeting the goal and give these tasks some clear dates. Remember that your goals should be specific, measurable, actionable, realistic, and time-based (S.M.A.R.T.).

Résumé Revamp

Now that you know more about how résumés should match up to job descriptions, you can write a more effective résumé that reflects your current standing in the job market. Consider revising chronological résumés by dropping old jobs, interests, or education that is not relevant to your current goals. If you haven't already done so, write a functional résumé that highlights the skills you've acquired.

Your Portfolio

Keep adding new elements to your portfolio. Some items you might include here are letters of recommendation, acknowledgments from others for contributions to their books, community- or service-based activities, and articles that you have written or that you've been quoted in. Add photos of menu items you've developed or that you've entered in competitions. Update your blogs with new entries that showcase your professional interests and accomplishments.

o   *Just like you do with your résumé, edit and proofread your information. Use proper, professional language and capitalization.*

o   *Do not use your work e-mail to set up or access your account. You may not have that e-mail forever, and the case could be made that if the account was made at work, utilizing a work e-mail, then all information on it (all of your contacts) belongs to your employer.*

New Stage, New Expectations, New Skills

The first stage of your career is spent building fundamental skills, gaining experience, and establishing professional connections. You learn to do the job and do it well. As you become more and more proficient, the next stage of your career begins to emerge. In this period, you begin to be asked to train, support, coach, and manage others. You may also look to focus your career in a more specific direction. Although you have built up a tremendous amount of practical and marketable skills to this point, you now are faced with the need to gain additional skills and/or credentials. You may need these skills to be able to do your job more effectively, or you may need a certain level of education or certification to apply for a higher-level position.

What They Really Mean: Developing Job Ad Intuition

During the first stage of your career, you probably asked many questions as you applied to jobs in order to gain an understanding of the expectations for a given position. The more you worked, the more you understood without having to ask those questions. You developed intuition. With a position title and a menu, you could reasonably determine what the job would entail.

In one sense, moving up means starting over. There is a learning curve as you identify and decode advertisements and expectations for the next level of position. Here is an example based on a management-level position, with the understanding that this same thought process transfers to any area of specialization.

Moving into a management position

EXAMPLE: ## Management Position

The following is a list of qualifications for a manager-in-training program for a hotel chain.

Applications for the Corporate Management Training Program are accepted throughout the course of the year for January and June placement. **Applicants must meet the following requirements in order to qualify for the program:**

○ *Bachelor's degree in a related field.*

- *Minimum GPA of 2.8.*

- *Nine months of relative industry work experience.*

- *Leadership and involvement in extracurricular activities and on-campus organizations.*

- *Positive references from two previous employers (no character references).*

- *Continuous authorization to work in the U.S.*

Initial Placement and Relocation

- *Placement in hotels is determined by the trainee's geographic preference and on participating hotel needs.*

[Hyatt Hotels]

This description provides some information explicitly, while some is implied and not stated outright. The ad lets you know that a certain degree level with specific GPA minimum is required. This means that applicants who do not meet these criteria will not be considered. How is this determined? The degree and GPA need to be both on your résumé and in the online application. What the ad does not tell you is that the application and materials will most likely be critiqued by an applicant tracking system, a type of software that screens candidates before humans see the applications. The desired criteria is input into the system, and the system searches the application materials for matching keywords. In this case, the software looks for the term *bachelor's*, rather than *BA*, *BS*, *BPS*, or any other set of initials. Notice that the ad only lists the level of degree, not the major.

Many of the other requirements are "specifically vague" — they give a general term without many qualifiers. "Nine months relevant work experience" as written indicates that any work experience in the hospitality industry or at a managerial level is acceptable. "Leadership and involvement in extracurricular activities and on-campus organizations" is also very vague. These items indicate minimums, but there is no indication of what makes one candidate more desirable than another. As you read a bit further into the advertisement, you find some clues: "Completion of the Corporate Management Training Program prepares trainees for a subsequent Assistant Manager– or Manager-level position in the division of the training concentration. For example, Operations trainees coming off the program may be placed as an Assistant Manager or Manager in the Housekeeping, Front Office, Reservations, Restaurants, or Banquets as a few possibilities. Culinary Trainees may be placed as Sous Chef, and Accounting Trainees as Credit Manager or Chief Accountant as possibilities."

If the end goal of the training program is to become assistant manager in a specific area, it follows that the most desirable applicants should have experience in the chosen area of concentration. Extracurricular activities and organizations should also have some related focus to make the candidate more desirable.

Candidates must present "Positive references from two previous employers (no character references)." These are written references from those in a position of authority who have directly observed your work. The references should mention how they know you, what position they held when you worked for them, how long you worked for them, and specific examples highlighting why you are a good candidate for this specific position. You know the hotel is looking for examples of leadership; it is in your best interest to have your reference writer highlight your leadership characteristics. You know this is a hotel chain, so there is most likely a mission statement, business philosophy, and brand image the hotel presents to the public. Have your references highlight your attributes in relation to this specific brand. Review the "References" drawer in your career filing cabinet. You may already have letters of recommendation that can be immediately used. If not, reconnect with those who have already written general recommendation letters for you and discuss the possibility of obtaining a new letter specific to this position.

Last, the advertisement speaks to geographical placement and the needs of the hotel. Yes, they are open to the candidate giving a specific location; however, that limits the opportunities available to the candidate. The most desirable candidates have geographic flexibility.

Although this ad gives some valuable specifics about requirements, it does not give you specific details about day-to-day responsibilities and expectations of either the training program or the end position of assistant manager. Before putting an application together, do some research. For instance, you can search for job listings for an assistant manager. Even if you aren't planning to apply to that specific company, you can learn some important things about the general expectations of applicants applying to become an assistant manager. Here is an example for an assistant food and beverage manager in a large hotel chain:

EXAMPLE:

Assistant Food and Beverage Manager

At _____, we believe our guests select _____ because of our caring and attentive associates who are focused on providing authentic hospitality and meaningful experiences to each and every guest. _____ is a place where high expectations aren't just met — they're exceeded. It's a place of outstanding rewards, where talent opens doors to exciting challenges in the hospitality industry.

_____ associates work in an environment that demands exceptional performance yet reaps great rewards. Whether it's career opportunities, job enrichment, or a supportive work environment, if you are ready for this challenge, then we are ready for you.

The Assistant Food and Beverage Manager oversees the food and beverage areas within the hotel. Responsibilities may include scheduling, forecasting and training, and ensuring compliance with federal, state, and local laws as well as all operating procedures. This person may also coordinate special events at the hotel. The Assistant Food and Beverage Manager must have strong communication and analytical skills. Food and Beverage cost control experience is helpful.

Qualifications:

○ *Minimum of 2+ years as F&B Management preferred.*

○ *Wine/beverage knowledge in an upscale environment preferred.*

○ *Ideal applicant should have strong organizational skills, ability to work with flexible work schedule, be a team player and a dynamic leader.*

Now that you know some of the requirements and qualifications for the end position (that is, the next higher position), you can use this information to focus your application. Notice that the description of how service is delivered to guests comes before the job description, demonstrating that the guest experience is the top priority. Everything in your application should match with this philosophy.

Applying This Information to a Bigger Picture

You have learned much about applying to this specific training program with this specific hotel chain. What if you do not want to apply here, to this position, or to a hotel? What if you do not see an advertisement but wish to prospect? The information here can be applied on a much wider scale. You can surmise that manager-in-training programs require a bachelor's degree. Maybe all do not, but there is a good chance they do and that your competition has that degree. The next higher position (assistant manager) prefers two years of management experience. "Prefers" indicates that candidates with this experience are most highly valued; however, they are open to the candidate demonstrating the value of their experience if they do not have two years. You can safely assume that the duties would be similar for any food and beverage management position, so you have some specific skill sets to highlight when applying.

It would be impossible to give this type of breakdown for every position. The details vary, but the technique of analyzing an advertisement and using it to craft your application materials to demonstrate that you are a desirable candidate remains the same. Essentially, this is the same process as in the foundational stage, except that you now have much more experience to draw upon as you craft your application materials.

Gaining or Honing New Skills

Inherent in career growth is the necessity to learn and apply new skill sets. Some of these occupationally related skills are "hard skills," such as learning new cooking methods, learning to complete a P&L statement, or learning to identify a grape variety through blind tasting. Cultivation of "soft skills," such as the ability to communicate effectively to varied audiences, resolve conflict, think strategically, and build effective teams, becomes increasingly

Achieving advanced certification

important as you move away from foundational types of positions. No longer are you just doing your job; you are also frequently called upon to ensure that others are doing their jobs, that individuals and teams are interacting effectively, that your ideas are being presented in a way so that they are heard, and that your bosses, coworkers, and customers are all happy. Two areas where those new to managing people may be immediately challenged are staffing and communication.

Gaining Credentials

As you research expectations and qualifications for the next move in your career, you may begin to notice that the positions you desire call for a level of education or a credential that you do not possess. Or perhaps you are rightly qualified for the next step, but the position two steps away requires a higher level of education or credentials. There are many cases where experience trumps education; however, if you do not have that extensive experience, and if the market is consistently demanding a specific credential, you have a decision to make. **If you are faced with the need to increase your credentials, consider the following:**

○ **Join professional organizations.** *The Research Chefs Association, American Culinary Federation, and Retail Bakers of America are examples of professional organizations offering certification programs. These formal programs allow you to demonstrate and document practical application of your knowledge.*

○ **Consider continuing education programs.** *These are intensive, short-term programs designed for the working professional to increase his or her knowledge.*

○ **Take a class.** *Check with your local community college. One class in management, statistics, writing, economics, chemistry, or another related subject boosts your knowledge, gets you back into "education" mode, and may be transferable if you decide to go on to the next level of degree.*

○ **Consider an online degree program,** *if your intended major would support that style of learning. Online programs are structured for working professionals. Review the school's accreditation — this is important because a school's accreditation must be recognized by the U.S. Department of Education in order to receive financial aid. In addition, proper accreditation makes the credits and degree earned "worth something," which is very important if you plan to pursue the next level of degree. You can find a list of the accrediting bodies recognized by the Department of Education by visiting the U.S. Department of Education's Web site.*

The CIA's Career Services Office receives more than 400 job postings each month. A surprisingly large number of them read something like this:

"_____ seeks _____.
Send resume to job@email.com."

Think about what this ad might be saying to the candidate. A lack of specific and descriptive information about the company (such as only listing "local restaurant franchise"), might send the message: "Our operation is so bad, if we told you the name you would not apply." On the other hand, a candidate might interpret the message this way: "We have not yet told our sous chef that he is going to be fired and we don't want him to know we are looking for the replacement." Perhaps a candidate will read it as saying: "We need help but don't want to put in the effort of actually speaking with potential candidates."

What type of candidates are these establishments expecting to recruit? Clearly, the employers are not positioning themselves to receive résumés from the very best candidates.

Job seekers are smart. Good ones will want to research your Web and social networking sites and ask friends for their take on your establishment so they can evaluate you. Top flight candidates want to arm themselves for an interview with this kind of information. A good ad means the difference between a great many mediocre candidates and the right number of well-qualified, excellent candidates.

Here are some simple ways to ensure that your ad attracts quality candidates:

- Give the name of the establishment. Would you honestly ever consider a candidate who gave you a résumé without a name on it? Your name is your brand, your moneymaker, so be proud of it!

- State the minimum qualifications and give a brief description of the job. Listing qualifications forces you, the employer, to know what you are looking for and allows you to narrow the pool of applicants quickly. Describing the position lets the candidates know what you expect. These descriptions are brief and they speak directly to the candidates you are looking for.

- Go where the right candidates are. Consider the more specialized sites for your ad placement. Culinary schools' recruiting systems such as HCareers, Chef and Restaurant Database, and HotelCareer might garner better-qualified candidates than posts on general job boards like Monster or Hotjobs.

- Review and hold onto résumés. If you see potential in a candidate but that person is not a good fit for the current opening, make a note. When you have openings in the future, reach out to old applicants. This can save you from posting another ad and starting the process again from scratch. Before posting an ad, have someone read it, and ask, "Based on these words alone, do you have enough information to determine whether you want to apply for the position?"

- ○ **Research traditional degree programs.** *As with online education, traditional programs are only as valuable as their accreditation. Use this Department of Education database to determine if a target school is accredited: http://ope.ed.gov/accreditation/Search.aspx.*

- ○ **If you do decide to enroll in a degree program,** *remember to fill out your FAFSA (financial aid form) and communicate with the school's financial aid office regarding scholarships and grants that may be available.*

Hiring Staff

As a job seeker, you tend to view the hiring process one-dimensionally; your primary concerns are all about you: How will you present yourself? How will this job affect your own well-being? You try to make employment decisions based upon what best benefits you. When you are called upon to make staffing decisions for your employer, you see the process from a different dimension. You have to make the best decision for the organization as a whole. You have to look at individuals and assess whether they are a good investment of your company's resources. You need to consider how you will be able to communicate both good and bad news to a potential employee.

It is beyond the scope of this book to instruct on best practices for hiring, training, coaching, retaining, and terminating employees. We can, however, provide some general guidelines to assist as you switch your point of view about the job search process from that of the job seeker to that of the person making hiring decisions.

- ○ **Identify your needs, and the reasons for them.** *Does the position need to be filled immediately? Can the workload be handled by the current staff, and if so, for how long? Are you replacing someone who is no longer with the company? Is this a new position? Does filling the position require a person of greater, less, or equal skill level than the previous worker? Include the "why" for each answer, because you will most likely have to make your case to your superior.*

- Identify the essential and desired qualifications for the position, *including education, experience, and skill sets, and the reasons why the candidates should possess these traits. Write them down. Knowing what you are looking for before you begin to look makes identifying the correct candidate easier. In addition, having written criteria helps protect you and your employer in a litigious society.*

- If you are posting an advertisement for the opportunity, *remember that it is an advertisement. You are selling your company as a desirable place to work. Use clear, concise language to communicate some information about the position, the employer, and your expectation of candidates' qualifications. Think of this advertisement as a résumé for your company.*

- Evaluate all applicants against your written criteria. *Think objectively and use your time wisely. View each application as an indication of future job performance. Did the applicant call when you explicitly requested contact via e-mail? If the position calls for "excellent communication skills," consider whether or not the applicant's résumé was difficult to read. It is probably wise not to spend time interviewing applicants who have not followed directions when there are others, equally qualified, who have.*

- When interviewing, pay attention to the whole person. *There are probably several other tasks that you need to be doing, but during an interview, your focus is on the applicants. It is their time. Are they maintaining eye contact? Do they handle difficult questions with grace and honesty? Are they trying to be likeable? Are they dressed appropriately for the position? Are they asking questions and interviewing you as well?*

Supervising Staff

As you grow in your career, you will find yourself in positions that call upon you to operate as the leader of a team of individuals. If your work has been self-directed up to this point, you may find that it is difficult to transition from the jack-of-all-trades chef to a supervisor in charge of a crew that includes cooks, sales staff, bartenders, and dining room staff. Keep these tips in mind as you grown into supervisory positions:

○ **Remember that not everyone has to be an expert at everything.** *Look for individuals who balance each other well. The goal of a manager is to ensure that the team is working for the good of the company.*

○ **Offer praise in public and blame in private.** *Work is stressful, especially when things go wrong. If a corrective conversation needs to take place, have it as quickly as possible and in private.*

○ **Realize that you are working with humans.** *We all have good points and shortcomings, good days and bad. Treat each employee fairly, as an individual. Listen, empathize, and make the best decisions for the good of the company.*

○ **Admit and take ownership of your mistakes.**

○ **Document everything.** *Every meeting with an applicant, every word of praise or corrective conversation, every incident or injury, should be recorded as part of your daily operations. If you have to have a difficult conversation with an employee about a situation that might lead to specific disciplinary action or termination, you should still have the conversation in private, but consider having another member of the management team present. Documentation helps to protect you and your employer, and another manager's presence validates your account of an incident and can help to diffuse an emotionally charged situation.*

○ **If you have to terminate, have your documentation in order.** *If termination is the only option, have a desk or table between yourself and the employee. Know your exits. Alert security if this is an option. Remember that you are not making a personal judgment about the individual; you are making a necessary decision about job performance.*

Communicating

During your foundational experiences, your workplace communication had been primarily between you, your co-workers, and your supervisors about the immediate aspects of your job. The circle of communication widens in terms of audience and subject matter as you grow in your career. Transitioning to a position of authority places you in a nexus of communication between your direct reports, other departments, your superiors, and your customers. You will need to effectively present ideas (yours or others') to superiors to enact change and convincingly present ideas (yours or others') to your direct reports to ensure that change happens.

Listening Effectively

You communicate most effectively when you listen effectively. You achieve more respect, gain more knowledge, and exert more influence when you listen to those around you. Listening effectively is not just waiting for a turn to speak; it is focusing on, acknowledging, and processing what another is saying without judgment. In the hospitality industry, you continually do this with your guests. You treat guests as individuals, focus on their concerns, demonstrate that you are listening through verbal and nonverbal cues, verbalize the correct response (a solution to a problem, for example), perform any necessary action, thank them for their input and business, and follow up with them to ensure you have meet their needs. Apply these same skills to your interactions with your co-workers and supervisors.

Effective listening begins with attention. Directing your attention toward the speaker not only helps you to focus on what is being said, but it also eases the speaker and creates an environment in which he or she can speak freely. This can be difficult. At any given moment, there are a thousand things that you need to do, and a conversation may not be high on your list. Remember, a position of leadership means that your responsibility is to make sure the team is functioning. A conversation now is an investment in productivity for later. **To show that you are listening:**

o **Stop what you are doing.**

o **Turn your body toward the speaker.**

o **Maintain eye contact.**

o **Nod your head and say "Yes," "Okay," "Go on," and so forth.**

- ○ **Be aware of your body language.** *If your arms are crossed and you are scowling, you have not created an environment conducive to communication.*

- ○ **Be quiet.** *Let the speaker speak. Resist any urge to interrupt, argue a point, or offer a solution before the speaker is done.*

What are you listening for?

- ○ **The true topic.** *Sometimes people have difficulty directly addressing an item that is bothering them. They may come to you with an issue about a specific incident; however, the true issue may be much deeper, and the incident was just the last straw.*

- ○ **The meaning behind their words.** *Employees and supervisors may be very emotional when they are speaking. It is important to acknowledge their feelings; however, it is also important that you not be distracted by their feelings so that you can truly understand the root of the issue.*

After they have spoken, paraphrase what they said to clarify that you have understood them correctly.

Respond appropriately. Acknowledge the speaker's feelings and thank the person for speaking with you. Then you should take whatever action is warranted. If it is appropriate, you may take immediate steps to address the situation. Other options might be to seek more information, request a follow-up meeting, or establish a date to update the individual.

Invite a response. This is another way of ensuring that you have understood the issue correctly and have addressed it. The challenge, of course, is that the appropriate solution may not be the solution the speaker had in mind or desires. While conflict resolution is beyond the scope of this book, Appendix IV includes a list of some of the resources available that can help you improve your listening and conflict resolution skills (see page 260).

Communicating Information

When you were a child, your parents, teachers, coaches, and other authority figures could motivate and convey the necessity of actions with the phrase "Because I said so!" This may work with children; however, it is not an effective means of communicating with other adults. Whether you are training a subordinate, collaborating with a peer, or promoting your ideas to your superiors, make your communications more effective by focusing on these three areas: attention, information, and understanding.

Information cannot be shared effectively unless the listener is focused enough to receive it. It is primarily the responsibility of the communicator to gain the focus and attention of the listener. Just because something is important to you does not mean it is equally important to others. **To create an environment where communication can happen:**

○ **Be aware of timing.** *There are times when a conversation is not an option. Let the other person know that you need to have a conversation and then find a mutually agreeable time so both of you can focus on the discussion.*

○ **Give the other person a reason to listen.** *Demonstrate why the topic is important. Create a connection and show the person the benefit.*

○ **Altering your speaking voice will gain attention.** *This does not mean screaming, although speaking loudly can work to your advantage when used sparingly. Speaking a bit more slowly and in a slightly lower tone than your usual speaking voice sends the message that what you are saying is important.*

Having gained the attention of your audience (even one person is an audience), you have to have something to say that will keep their attention. Consider your audience as you prepare to communicate the essential information.

- **Organize your information so that it makes sense to your audience.** *Use a logical progression (A to B to C) so that your audience can easily follow your train of thought. Break down complex information into smaller parts, and draw connections between topics to demonstrate interrelationships.*

- **Vary the presentation of your information to best suit your audience and keep interest.** *When training someone, demonstrate and talk through each task at the same time. If using presentation software, use the visuals and your spoken information to complement each other, rather than just reading the words on the screen verbatim.*

- **Know your audience.** *Adjust your presentation method to best suit your audience. Some groups respond well to facts and figures; include tables, charts, or graphs to get important information across. Some people like to take notes, especially if the presentation includes instructions or action steps; pause often to allow them to get the key points down on paper. Impeccable timing and stellar presentations do not count for much if your audience does not understand the information you have presented.*

Check for understanding by:

- *Asking your audience to summarize what you have told them.*

- *Asking your audience to demonstrate the task you have shown them.*

- *Asking your audience probing questions about the information and encouraging them to ask questions.*

Knowing When to Make Your Next Career Move

According to a Bureau of Labor Statistics report, as of January 2010, the median number of years employees had been with their current employer was 4.4 years. This length of time, called *tenure*, changes drastically based on the age of the individual: Younger people change jobs more frequently than older people. Those aged 20 to 24 years old average 1.5 years at each job, whereas workers in the 55-to-64 age group average 10 years at each employer. If you liberally apply the average tenure of 4.4 years to an individual who begins working full-time (meaning that work, not education, is their primary responsibility) at age 22 after graduating college, and who works until age 65, a total of forty-three years, that person will have approximately ten jobs during his or her career.

Some of these changes are planned, calculated, and amicable partings in line with an individual's career goals. Some are sudden, beyond the individual's control, not by choice, and not on the best of terms. It is in your best interest, as a job seeker, to hope for the best and plan for the worst by remaining vigilant for opportunities, reflecting upon and updating your goals, and maintaining strong networking ties.

Individuals and individual situations vary greatly. The decision to change jobs is a major one, and there are multiple factors, both direct and collateral, that contribute to this decision.

Preliminary Questions

Here are some considerations to ponder when you begin to wonder if it is time to move on.

○ *Have you reviewed your goals? How is your current position helping you to get to where you want to be five years from now? Have you achieved the goals you had set when you took your current position?*

○ *Are you running toward something or running away from something? Meaning, are you looking to leave your current position out of anger or spite, or are you leaving because you are pursuing the next stage of your career?*

○ *Have you formulated the goals you are aspiring to achieve from your next move?*

○ *Do you have the skill sets, education, or depth of experience needed to take the next step?*

○ *Have you spoken with your mentor or trusted contacts to gain others' perspectives on your current situation?*

○ *Have you estimated the potential costs of changing jobs? You will want to consider the costs of relocation; any lag between paychecks from the last check at the old job and the first check at the next; transportation and parking costs; changes in commuting time; costs of clothing for new uniforms or work clothes; changes to health coverage and retirement savings; and tuition for additional education.*

As chef and restaurateur Grant Achatz explained in a presentation to students in April 2011, "As long as you feel you are still growing, you should stay [in your current position]. If you feel that you have plateaued out or hit a ceiling for whatever reason, it is time to move on. Work really hard to build a foundation, then jump. Hit the next pad and jump again."

It Is Time. Now What?

Once you have decided it is time to move on, there are three major areas to address:

---

1. *What are you looking to do?*

---

2. *What is your strategy?*

---

3. *How are you going to handle your current employment?*

Let's look at number three first, because it has the most significant impact on your current situation.

When you begin to look for a new opportunity, it makes sense that you will use your network to ask for references or inquire about opportunities. You may speak with your friends, some of whom may be colleagues. You may need to take time off from work to go to an interview. You can bet that your current employer will find out that you are looking elsewhere, and this can lead to an uncomfortable situation, especially if you are looking for work at a business that is a direct competitor. In an ideal world, if you have done consistently good work, your employer will be supportive of your growth and act as a resource during your search. You will need to assess your own situation and decide how much information you are comfortable with sharing, as well as at what point in your search you are comfortable sharing this information. Some employers will be an ally as you plot your career path, even if it means you are leaving them. Others may feel betrayed.

If you feel that it is reasonable, try to establish an honest, positive discussion with your current employer early on. Since they will find out you are looking elsewhere regardless, it is generally better to have the conversation and let your search be in the open than to try to hide your search. Although no one wants to see solid performers leave their team, part of being a manager is building up your team members and being willing to let them go to pursue their own directions. Are there managers who will become angry when they find out that their employees are looking elsewhere? Of course. However, if you have cultivated a relationship with your manager, meaning that you have performed well and have interacted with him or her about your career goals, then your manager is more likely to understand your situation and be willing to help you move on and move up.

Determining Your Next Move

Even with a solid base of experience, changing jobs means starting over. Once you have taken a new position, you have a new employer, new co-workers, and new skill sets to learn. The decision to leave your current job and the decision to accept a new position should be made with a purpose in mind. They should, in some way, be decisions that advance your career. Before deciding to leave one position, it is essential that you reflect on your past, look to your future, and then ask, "What do I want to do?"

Look back on the goals you had set earlier in your career. Having gained foundational experience, you most likely have completed many of your short-term goals. Those goals that were, at the time, intermediate goals may now be more immediately attainable, so they become your new short-term goals. You may be able to more clearly see and define the steps that separate your current position and your ultimate goal. That allows you to generate new intermediate goals. Perhaps you did not have a clear long-term direction when starting out. Now, with some experience, your long-term vision may be clearer. Alternatively, perhaps you are considering a different direction for your career than you had previously, such as entrepreneurship, consultation, or a radical shift requiring new foundational education and experiences, and it is time to start creating a completely new set of goals. Remember that goals are guidelines, providing meaning, structure, and support; they can and should adapt as your career evolves.

Developing Your Strategy

This is a time for research. As you begin to formulate your next move, use your current network and create new connections to gain a clear picture of what that new ideal position entails, such as skills required, day-to-day responsibilities, additional certifications/education, and so on. Review this information and identify areas where you are strong and areas where growth prior to changing positions would make you more desirable. Some growth may be possible at your current position.

For many people the journeyman stage is the time in their career when they are first expected to manage others. However, positions that call for management may often include a requirement for prior management experience. Job seekers are faced with an age-old question: How do I get the job when I need experience to get the job, but I need the job to get the experience? The answer to this question lies in the term *experience*. If you do not have a documented background with a specific job skill set, you need to identify those traits/experiences/skills that the position demands. If you want to demonstrate that you are capable of moving into a management position, you can look for traits you have in common with managers. **After you read advertisements for management positions, you can identify that managers:**

- *Have a working understanding of and familiarity with the jobs of the individuals they are managing.*

- *Have a clear understanding of the goals of the business, how that business works to achieve those goals, and the ability to ensure that direct reports are working to meet these goals in the way that the business wants them met.*

- *Have the ability to build strong teams by hiring the correct individuals; coaching team members to improve performance; identifying areas of strength and weakness within their team members; creating an environment that allows for synergy between team members; and removing team members who are not performing to expectations.*

- *Have a clear understanding of financial responsibility.*

- *Have the ability to communicate effectively and appropriately to a wide range of audiences, including direct reports, external customers, and upper management.*

- *Possess the ability to identify problem areas for the business and the vision to create and implement solutions to these problems.*

- *May have achieved specific educational requirements, depending upon the employer.*

This information provides you with a baseline to create a strategy for applying for a management position. Identify areas in your current and past positions where you were called upon to demonstrate these traits. Highlight them prominently in your résumé, on your online social/professional networking platforms, and to your network. Are there any opportunities within your current position where you can gain or demonstrate some of these skills? For instance, can you train new hires or contribute to the interview process? Can you cost out recipes, examine workflow, or assist with inventory to demonstrate financial accountability? Can you bring in new ideas (for a special, for a new wine, or for a new promotion to build the business), present them professionally, implement them, and track their success to demonstrate that you are able to contribute to the business as a whole?

Are there areas where you do not meet the criteria whatsoever? These are areas of possible resistance. The challenge here is to fight the urge to qualify your experience when faced with resistance. "But," "although," and "even though" are examples of qualifiers, as in "I do not have that experience, but . . ." or "Although I do not have the required degree. . . ." Rather than taking this approach, demonstrate positive, tangible steps that you have taken toward building up those areas where you are lacking.

Does the position require a degree that you do not have? You can begin by taking a single course online or at a community college to demonstrate that you are advancing your knowledge. Never been called upon to help build a team? There were most likely numerous times when you assisted a new hire with learning the job and intuitively knew whether or not that person would work out. Think about how you did this and actually write down what you did, what has worked, and what has not. Now you are able to demonstrate your training/coaching methods.

Review the résumé, interviewing, and networking techniques described in chapters 3 and 4. Apply the techniques described to your current information and situation to create a self-marketing system that sells you to the position you are seeking. Perhaps a change in your résumé style from straight chronological to a hybrid of chronological and functional would be beneficial. With this style, you can focus the reader's attention toward applicable skill sets and accomplishments and away from job titles. The same strategy can be used when changing careers. Highlight your transferable skills. These are the universal skills that are valuable regardless of job title or industry segment. They draw the reader's attention to your abilities rather than your job titles.

Does this sound like spin and strategy? Yes, it is. In truth, whenever you look to move to a higher position, you are selling yourself on your potential because you have not done that job before. A large part of the job seeker's success comes from effectively demonstrating potential. You may face resistance, but you should prepare in advance for it and have confidence in the abilities and skills you have acquired throughout your career.

Exiting Gracefully

Common wisdom tells us that people remember most clearly the last piece in a series of events. In order to maintain a positive relationship with an employer, it is important to leave a position on a positive note. An accepted employment practice for an hourly employee is to give two weeks notice when deciding to leave a position. This notice should be given both verbally and in writing to your direct supervisor, and, of course, you should follow any other procedures that your current employer requires. More time is generally given for salaried (upper-level) positions since it is more difficult to fill these positions. If you are under contract, carefully review the terms

What if the Decision to Leave is Not Yours?

As much as you would like every career move to be well planned, controlled, and beneficial, there are times when a move is not any of these things. You may face layoffs, closings, dangerous situations, and even situations when you are responsible for unfortunate decisions that lead to termination. When these situations arise, the job search process becomes much more urgent, with much less time for reflection, planning, and strategizing.

No matter how good an employee you are, none of us are so essential that we cannot be replaced. This should not be your primary thought throughout the day; however, you should always be prepared to make a move.

○ Remain aware of your current situation. Watch business levels. Listen when management speaks. Observe changes in hiring practices, changes in pricing, and changes in day-to-day operations.

○ Remain aware of your employer's competition. How is their business doing? Are you gaining from them or losing to them? Are they hiring people or laying them off, changing their prices, or changing their marketing strategies?

○ Monitor job boards and professional networking groups. Be aware of other opportunities.

○ Keep your résumé updated. We advise job seekers to "never be more than five feet from your résumé," because you never know. E-mail it to yourself so that you can access it from any Internet connection. Update your LinkedIn profile and send invitations to connect at every opportunity.

○ Keep your network strong. Remain in contact with your connections. Create relationships with your vendors and delivery drivers. They are in five, ten, or as many as twenty places every day. It helps their business if they can get their customers good employees.

○ Use your common sense. Not showing up for work and failing to call will usually result in immediate

of your contract with your legal counsel before making any decisions about terminating that contract.

During the period of your notice, work as hard as or harder than you would normally. Giving in to "short-timer syndrome" will leave your employer, manager, and co-workers with the impression that you do not care about them or the business, even if your entire tenure of employment has been exemplary. Obtain letters of reference from your management team, and collect contact information from management, your co-workers, and vendors so that they can remain an active part of your network. Be sure to return any items that belong to the company, and be sure to say good-bye to everyone before you leave.

termination. Theft can get you fired, and in addition, you may find yourself arrested and thrown in jail. Harassment and abuse or bad-mouthing your employer or co-workers will get you fired (and probably sued). Testing positive in a drugfree workplace will get you fired on the spot. If you are given a second chance, learn your lesson and never repeat the behavior. You have control over these behaviors and you alone are responsible for your poor choices. If you are fired for any of these reasons, your road back to employment may be longer than it would be for someone who was laid off due to a decline in business.

If you do lose your job suddenly, begin to apply to new positions immediately. This is not the time to begin looking for that dream position; this is a time for action. It is advisable to take any position that will provide you income and work history. Swallow any sense of pride that may prevent you from taking an available opportunity. This will most likely be a temporary position providing income (maybe not at the level you were used to, but some income is better than no income) and work history.

Beyond being able to meet life's responsibilities, there is a very significant reason for being employed in any capacity: Studies have shown that the longer someone is out of work, the less likely it is that that person will be hired in the future.

If you become unemployed, take a job — any job — so that you can pursue another position that is more directly in line with your career goals. Gain employment first, then regroup, reflect, and look to move forward. Use any time you are out of work to better yourself: Continually apply to jobs, take a class, start a blog, or cater your friend's party. Keep yourself actively involved with your job search and actively involved with life. A termination is not a statement on your character, and even if it was due to a mistake on your part, you can still learn from it. Remain positive about your overall experience rather than focusing on the negative circumstances surrounding your departure.

Some employers will not accept your notice for whatever reason. A distributor may terminate a member of the sales team immediately when that member gives notice, because the company fears the employee may leave with client information or become irresponsible with accounts receivable. This is unfortunate, but it may be unavoidable. Know that you have done the right thing by giving notice, and remain confident that your management team, co-workers, and clients will recognize and recommend you based upon your history of solid performance.

Summary

Effective career management means that you are constantly preparing yourself for the next job, with the express purpose of landing that new position. If you are determined to grow a career, even if you are gainfully and happily employed in your current position, you can and should showcase your career, accomplishments, skills, and experiences. You may not think you are in the market for a new position, but someone else may be ready to approach you, if that person can see your potential.

The transition from novice to journeyman is a process of demonstrating that you have the potential to learn new skills, take on new demands, and meet (and exceed) the new expectations that are the standards in higher-level positions. Some aspects of preparing yourself for the next level, such as obtaining a degree, constitute a significant investment of your time, while others, such as learning to communicate effectively, can be incorporated into what you are already doing by simply creating opportunities to practice skills.

If you are constantly aware of what you want your next move to be and what that position will demand, you can take the steps necessary to prepare yourself. Remain active and visible within your organization and your profession and continue to build your network so that when opportunities arise you not only know where to find them, but you also know that you are positioned to take advantage of them.

Exercises

Exercise 1:   ## Creating a Bio

By this stage in your career you have created numerous résumés, perhaps in a variety of formats. These work well for job applications; however, as you begin to move further toward being a "master," there will be times when a résumé is not the ideal way to provide information about yourself. You may be listed on the "About Us" section of your company's or your own Web page and promotional material, contribute to a publication, or be featured at an event. A biographical sketch is more effective in these situations. A bio tells your story briefly, in a friendly and conversational manner. Bios are written in the third person (using your name rather than "I") and generally do not include the hard data (dates, numbers, percents, and so on) that is found in a résumé. Write a bio that tells the story of you, in one page or less.

Exercise 2:   ## Expanding Your Network

By this point you should have established a LinkedIn profile, and you may be a member of one or more professional organizations. Take advantage of the discussion groups on LinkedIn or on your professional organizations' Web sites. Start a discussion and comment on ongoing discussions. Use these virtual tools to interact regularly with other like-minded professionals.

seven

THE MASTER CULINARIAN

IF YOU HAVE BEEN DILIGENT about writing, reviewing, and applying your goals throughout your career, there will come a day when you reach a position of influence and authority — you will be a master culinarian. The exact title you hold may be chef-owner, noted entrepreneur, lead position in a research and development kitchen, chef-instructor, executive chef or pastry chef, food and beverage director, master sommelier, author, media personality, or consultant, to name a few.

The true measure of whether or not you have achieved mastery is not necessarily the size of your salary — although there is no shame in expecting that as you grow in your career, your salary will reflect your increasing worth. It is more likely that you will have learned your own measures of mastery along the way. Now you have the right and the responsibility to ensure the continuing advancement of the culinary arts. You may find that mastery in one area is an encouragement to take up a new goal or to continue to move up within a company or corporation by taking on some new challenges.

Reinventing Your Career

"Where do I go from here?" This question occurs in cycles. It was asked as you started out. It was asked when you were ready to move up from novice to journeyman. And now, at the third stage of your career, that of a "master," having enjoyed success as an influential professional, you are at a point where you are reaching what were once long-term goals. For many, new

If you are considering opening your own business, the Small Business Administration provides immensely valuable resources, including a preparation checklist, a template to create a business plan, ways to find financing, and links to identify which licenses/permits/paperwork you will need to obtain in your specific location. The Small Business Administration's Web site is a great place to start.

Entrepreneurs do not need to be expert at every element of the business. They do, however, need to be expert at identifying complementary resources. There are those who have great, potentially profitable ideas but no aptitude for finances. Others may be incredibly motivating speakers who are better at presenting others' ideas than coming up with their own. Some make magic with numbers yet are terrified to speak in front of a group. The most successful entrepreneurs identify their own strengths and weaknesses, and the strengths and weaknesses of others, then create teams that are stronger than the sum of their parts. Remember, the business needs to sustain itself. In order to do this, the entrepreneur has to let go once in a while, trusting that the team he or she has built will continue to drive the business forward according to plan. Letting other experts execute the day-to-day operations while you engage in long-term planning is a difficult yet necessary skill to master.

challenges keep us going. But what happens when you have worked to achieve success in an upper-level position and there is nowhere else to go, and when a lateral move would mean only a change in details without affording the potential for further growth?

This is a stage when many seek to redefine themselves, either with a major directional shift or by engaging in side projects. In many ways, starting fresh is very similar in nature to when you started as a novice culinarian, beginning with identifying an end point and creating short-term, intermediate, and long-term goals appropriate to your new direction. The main difference is that you now have valuable, measurable, and documented experiences and a strong, viable network; both can, and should, be used to your advantage.

Preparation, promotion, and persistence are three building blocks that support successful people, and we will explore each in this chapter.

Preparation

Throughout your career, you have gained knowledge, skills, and experiences that have allowed you to progress. As you look to redefine your career, the effect of your experiences becomes part of your credentials. For instance, the success of a restaurant consultant is not solely based on knowledge of cuisine; success is also based on the application of that knowledge: identifying trends and how to apply those trends to increase business; identifying and understanding why an operation does or does not run smoothly and creating systems that will increase efficiency; and identifying purveyors, equipment, and potential hires that cost the least and contribute the most to that business's success.

Turning the analytical skills that have contributed to your success on yourself may illuminate areas where further preparation is needed before undertaking a new venture. The next higher degree may be required to break through a ceiling. Intimate knowledge of cuisine, trends, and operations does not directly translate into being a successful salesperson, educator, or business owner. Taking a class or studying books by knowledgeable authors will be of great value. Taking time to *stage* (yes, just like when you were a novice) under specialists, trend makers, and high-level professionals will increase your knowledge and provide you with new, fresh ideas to increase business.

A significant consideration is that established professionals cannot just step away from their professional and personal responsibilities. Time management and return-on-investment analysis, two skills that have contributed to your professional success, need to be applied to your career decisions. "What am I going to get out of this?" and "How much time can I realistically devote to it?" are intertwining and essential questions. **Considerations to prepare for a major move when you are well into your career include:**

○ **Am I prepared/able to face a drop in income due to increased expenses** (*continuing education, start-up costs for a new business*) *and/or a reduction in pay resulting from entering a new field at a lower level than my current position?*

○ **What are the expenses associated with this move,** *and what is the projected long-term return? Can I realistically recoup the expense of pursuing a terminal degree considering the amount of time left in my career? Will the change lead to a better quality of life, and is a temporary disruption worth the long-term benefit?*

○ **Am I physically, mentally, and emotionally able to commit to this move?** *Owning a business, for instance, is a 24/7 job. Entering a new field may involve taking direction and criticism rather than giving direction and criticism, and becoming the novice when you have been the expert. Obtaining additional education requires an immense investment of time to attend classes (even virtually) and complete homework, which will put more strain on an already tight schedule.*

○ **Are there alternatives that may yield the same results?** *Can I remain at my current position, which may not be as fulfilling and rewarding as it once was, and take on side ventures rather than completely leaving a sure thing and leaping into the unknown? For example, you could consider investing in a business rather than commanding the day-to-day operations, turning a hobby into a minor moneymaker, or working part- rather than full-time in a new field.*

Master Stage Applications

The fundamentals behind applying for a job do not change as you progress in your profession; however, some of the details do. Earlier in your career, the challenge was to rise to the top of a vast pool of similarly qualified applicants. As the level of the job increases, the pool of available and qualified talent decreases. The risks are also greater for both applicant and employer: High-level positions are vital to maintaining and increasing the business's position in the market; the candidate must be able to learn quickly and demonstrate immediate results. These positions are expensive, so there must be measurable return on investment. These are high-stress positions; candidates must be able to gather information, synthesize data, calculate risk, and implement solutions quickly; they must be able to lead, delegate, and communicate with a wide variety of personality types; and they must be able to accept blame from internal and external sources.

Although the details of the application and interview process for upper-level positions are highly situational based upon the position and the company, there are several universal points to be aware of.

○ **Upper-level positions are responsible for moving the business forward.** *Demonstrate in your résumé, cover letter, and interview that you know and understand the business. Research beyond the "About Us" tab on their Web site. Know the history, strengths, struggles, and people. Refer to their mission statement, organizational goals, and philosophy.*

○ **Demonstrate that you have internalized the mission statement.** *You will be serving as an example to your workers and customers; your face will be associated with the employer's brand. Highlight this all the way through the application process.*

○ **Effective written and verbal communication are essential skills.** *Display these skill sets through the application process.*

○ **All applicants will have relatively the same qualifications.** *Leaders deliver results. Showcase both the solutions you have implemented and the* thought processes behind their creation. Demonstrate that you have developed your team members up, and in some cases, out to greater success. Highlight your ability to effectively manage the most precious resource — time.

- ○ **Be honest and candid.** *You will most likely be interviewing with multiple people. The interviewers will confer with each other. Inconsistent answers will raise red flags. The interviewers are not looking for the answer you think they want to hear; they are looking for your answer. Own success and failure as learning and growth experiences.*

- ○ **Silence is acceptable.** *Some interviewers will actually use silence to see if it unnerves the candidate and causes him or her to begin babbling. If the interviewer goes silent, use the opportunity to ask questions. If you are faced with a difficult question, take some time to process it. Quick answers can come off as rehearsed responses.*

- ○ **You may be required to take a personality test.** *Don't be fazed by this; answer the questions without analyzing them. These tests are used to validate personality types/traits the interviewer sees and to get past the initial façade that many applicants wear to interviews. If something in the results is brought up as a potential negative — for instance, a trend toward introversion may appear as a negative for a position requiring heavy client interaction — turn it into a positive. A response to this example might be: "I can understand this result. I am not a social butterfly, nor do I tend toward chattiness. I listen rather than waiting to speak, which allows me to hear, understand, and process the client's needs and create solutions that meet and exceed that individual's needs."*

Age in the Job Search

According to a March 2010 Bureau of Labor Statistics report, unemployed workers age 55 and over remained unemployed for an average of 35.5 weeks, compared to 30.3 weeks for 25 to 54 year olds, 23.3 weeks for 16 to 24 year olds, and 29.3 weeks for those aged 16 and under. This statistic does not seek to identify *why* this variation exists, only to show that there is a difference. Federal law prohibits discrimination based upon age. Anecdotal information indicates that some are concerned that their age has been a reason for not receiving an offer.

If you feel that your age has become a limiting factor in your job search, it is extremely important to refocus your perception to believe that the skills and experiences you have gained throughout your career are beneficial. You simply will not be able to sell yourself as a benefit if you do not first believe in yourself. Too often, insecurity and thinking negatively about an outcome leads to the realization of that outcome. The good news is that the reverse also holds true: Positive thoughts and actions (both need to be present) lead to increased positive results.

After addressing self-perception, the next item to consider is your qualifications versus the types of employment you are pursuing. As with any job search, if you are not meeting the minimum qualifications, you probably will not go far in the process. If you are pursuing positions for which you are rightly qualified and have successfully completed part of the hiring process (that is, you have been interviewed, perhaps several times) but have not been given offers, you need to consider that perhaps the competition is better suited to the position than you are. Remember, as a candidate, you are not privy to your competition's application process, so you cannot compare and judge your application process against your competition.

If you do feel that age, rather than qualifications and quality of competition, is a factor, let's think about why age would concern a potential employer in the first place. **Some perceived concerns might be:**

○ *An older worker may not be aware of current trends, technology, and so forth.*

○ *An older worker's experience might make him or her expensive, especially if that worker is changing career directions. (The employer may think, "How can I pay someone an entry-level salary who has that level of degree/ experience?")*

○ *An older worker might not have the stamina to do the job.*

○ *An older worker may be set in his or her ways and not easily trained.*

○ *An older worker may not take direction effectively from a younger supervisor.*

○ *An older worker may be close to retirement age and not committed to a long-term career with the company.*

The methods to combat these perceived or actual concerns are the same methods that are best practices for all job searches. Let's look at each of these points individually.

An older worker is not aware of current trends, technology, and so forth:

○ *If you are competing with younger workers who are fresh out of college, they often demonstrate that they are eager and willing and have many new ideas using the latest technologies and theories. You have demonstrated, measurable, and proven results that your solutions have worked. Focus on your results and the methodology used to achieve them.*

○ *Lead with a "Training and Education" section on your résumé and list applicable and recent training, certifications, and so on first.*

○ *Alter the language of your experience descriptions to use current jargon, mention your application of current trends to the business, and specifically indicate experience with pertinent computer programs and technology.*

An older worker's experience makes him or her expensive:

○ *If you are applying to positions that are comparable to or higher than your current position, in the same industry and geographical area, this is not an issue — you should expect a comparable or higher salary for the same or more demanding work.*

- *Know your market value and your salary threshold, and know the position's market value. If the two match up, there is no issue. If the position would be a pay cut, and you are willing and able to take that cut, emphasize this in your interview by stating something like "I understand this position is in this range [indicate range], and my last/current position was/is in this range [state range]. There is a discrepancy here. If I thought at any point it would be an issue, I would not have applied in the first place. This is why I am here. . . ."*

An older worker may not have the stamina to do the job:

- *Highlight your length of time in the industry. As an experienced professional, your "stamina" is measured in terms of years.*

- *If applying for a physically demanding job, seek to demonstrate that you have recently done the job.*

- *Demonstrate in all of your communications that you understand and are able to perform the requirements of the job.*

An older worker may not be easily trained:

- *Demonstrate your trainability by speaking of specific instances in which you have adapted to new situations and continued to provide the same or higher level of performance.*

- *Display your knowledge about how that employer does business to highlight that you have begun to understand and appreciate their methodology for getting things done.*

- *Indicate that you learn every day and are welcoming of new challenges.*

An older worker may not effectively take direction from a younger supervisor:

○ *This feeling is based on the assumption that an older, perhaps more experienced, worker will try to take the job of a younger superior. If you sense this attitude, create a nonthreatening environment by focusing on the job you are applying for, as opposed to presenting ideas that are more appropriate for the supervisor's level. Professionals respect their superiors regardless of age and understand that their job (at any level within the organization) is to drive business by doing their job well.*

An older worker may be close to retirement age and not committed to a long-term career with the company.

○ *"Retirement age" is no longer the universal age of 65 that it once was. Many people continue to work well past that age.*

○ *According to the Bureau of Labor Statistics' Employee Tenure Summary (September 14, 2010), "The median number of years that wage and salary workers had been with their current employer was 4.4 in January 2010." This indicates that workers do not tend to hold "long-term" positions with employers. However, "The length of time a worker remains with the same employer increases with the age at which the worker began the job." (BLS News Release, "Number of Jobs Held, Labor Market Activity, and Earnings Growth Among the Youngest Baby Boomers," September 10, 2010)*

As you can see, the solution to a concern about age is not to appear younger, but rather to present and own your value. At the end of the day, success is based upon delivering results, whether that is a certain profit margin or ensuring that every plate was served correctly and on time. Sell your proven results. You also have an extensive network. Utilize the connections you have developed. Let others champion your proven results.

Promoting your business and yourself

Promotion

"You have to bang the drum in life sometimes. God is already famous . . . but that does not stop the preacher from ringing the church bell every morning." —Paul Bocuse, CIA Chef of the Century

Having a high degree of skill and well-thought-out solutions to problems becomes the most beneficial to you when others know about them. Self-promotion is controlled bragging, the idea of which makes many feel uncomfortable. But in reality, it is no different from advertising for a product, service, or business. Remember, your competition is out there doing it. Potential bosses, investors, customers, clients, and employees will not intrinsically know how to find you or that you are of value; you need to inform them. You have already been doing this to some extent throughout your career: Résumés, portfolios, networking, blogs, and so on, all of which grew from your career filing cabinet, are self-promotional tools. At this stage, you are now seeking to position and promote yourself as an expert in your field, which requires different styles of communication to reach the appropriate audience.

Direct person-to-person recommendations are by far the best form of promotion; however, they will reach a relatively limited audience. The quickest, most cost-effective method of reaching the largest possible audience is use of the Web. If at any point you find yourself saying, "I don't understand it," "I can't keep up with it," "I don't have the time to play with that," or anything similar, then you and your business have lost out to your competition.

Web Site

Your Web site is your home base. It is the static façade of your business or brand. All of your social media, e-mail signatures, and printed materials will link back to this place. Because this is your virtual "face," it is a worthwhile investment to enlist the services of a professional Web developer. Before communicating with a developer, take some time to consider what message you are looking to communicate to your target audience. Refer to the section on presentations (see page 223), as many of the same thought processes apply.

When meeting with potential developers for your Web site, Donna Davies, Web marketing manager at The Culinary Institute of America, suggests the following:

1. *Pay attention to how much time they take in learning about you and your business. If they take no time at all, then you may end up getting a cookie-cutter design.*

2. *Look at their portfolio. Do all their designs look the same or are they different? A range of designs shows that they have the talent to be flexible.*

3. *Take note as to whether the work will be done by the agency or outsourced. This may affect the costs, and quality could be sacrificed if much of the work is to be outsourced.*

---

4. *Find out what their fee structure is, and get it in writing.*

---

5. *Speak with their existing clients. Inquire about their overall level of satisfaction during and after working with the developer. Ask the following questions: Did the developer accurately create your vision? Was the developer easy to work with (listened to your needs, returned calls/e-mails promptly, and so on)? Did the developer deliver the product on time and within budget? Has the developer remained available to you to troubleshoot issues with the site?*

Social Media

Social media makes it easy to find and communicate with people, businesses, and organizations. You can access it at home, at work, or from your phone. The promotional value of Facebook, Twitter, Flickr, and LinkedIn, to name only a few avenues, cannot be understated. Because these tools are by nature easily accessible to others, you must remember to use them to your benefit, not your disadvantage. Having a clearly defined strategy about how to use these tools will enable you to turn these free resources into revenue-generating assets.

○ **Decide on the image you desire to portray** *and maintain that image across all platforms.*

○ **Utilize different platforms for different purposes.** *If you are using Facebook to connect with friends and family, consider having a separate Fan Page for your business or you as a public figure. Professional and business acquaintances can be directed to communicate with you there rather than on another page where you would be sharing your personal life with them. Twitter is designed for quick headlines, so it is perfect to promote daily specials, job opportunities, interesting and useful tidbits, and so on. LinkedIn is a professional networking site. Use it to search for and connect with professionals, gather recommendations, or share your résumé. Flickr is a photo-sharing site that is perfect for promoting visuals.*

- **Post consistently.** *If you are not in your followers' news feeds, you will be forgotten.*

- **Work smartly.** *Use a system such as Twitter's TweetDeck, which can link all of your social applications, allowing you to send updates and monitor multiple platforms from one location. This and similar programs allow you to schedule updates, so you can compose multiple updates at one time and have them posted throughout the day.*

- **Connect your platforms.** *Have live links to your social media and static Web site on your e-mail signature. Ensure that each platform allows viewers to link to the others.*

- **Actively participate, through commenting and posting, in professional groups within social media sites.** *This exposes your name and expresses your thought leadership to a wider audience.*

Leadership in Professional Organizations and Events

Seek leadership positions in professional organizations. Attend their conferences, webinars, and chapter meetings to establish your presence, share your expertise, and network with those currently in leadership roles. Serve on committees and shape or write policy that will move the organization or profession forward. If you have a business, become a member of your local Chamber of Commerce. At every possible opportunity, shake hands, hand out your business card, and give your thirty-second elevator speech. When you receive business cards, send LinkedIn requests, become a fan of their Facebook page, and follow them on Twitter to keep that connection warm.

Persistence

Persistence is truly nothing more than continuous preparation and promotion regardless of success or failure. *Or* is the important word. Every one of us is a job seeker. If you are successful in meeting the right person, under the right circumstances, and you land the job you are after, there is no guarantee that you will still have that job tomorrow, so you must remain current and vigilant with your job-searching activities. If you meet with rejection or failure, you need to continue on. Yes, you need to analyze the reason for failure and learn from it; however, you cannot let failure plunge you into inaction. When one door fails to open, immediately try another.

Effective Leadership

In the last chapter, we spoke about effective communication, focusing upon person-to-person interactions. Managers interact directly with the team members who are working to meet a specific goal. They are supplying the answers concerning *how* to do things. Leaders, by contrast, may find themselves communicating with a much wider audience. The message that they have to share is fundamental to the success of an operation because it answers the questions about *why* the business should be doing something. In order to get these important messages across, leaders can use a variety of tactics. One of the most common is a presentation.

Presentations

A presentation is at the same time an extension of and an entity independent from individual communication. Earlier in your career you attended meetings and presentations; now you are expected to call meetings and give presentations. Speaking in front of a group, large or small, can be intimidating; however, as you grow in your career, these activities are not optional. They become part of your day-to-day duties. Chefs conduct preservice meetings, educating the service staff on the daily specials and training them on how to sell these items to the guests. An entrepreneur presents a business plan to potential investors. An educator presents the daily lessons to students. An executive presents updates about the company to its employees and board members. Presentations are an opportunity to teach, inspire, and gain support, all of which are among the duties of a leader.

Presentations consist of three components: verbal (the words that are spoken), vocal (the manner of your speech), and visual (how you look when you are speaking). **According to the American Hotel & Lodging Educational Institute, the overall impact of a presentation is divided among these three components as follows:**

Giving effective presentations

Verbal: 7%
Vocal: 38%
Visual: 55%

You can see by this breakdown that the actual information you are seeking to convey has a small impact, the quality of your voice has a much greater impact, and how you carry yourself when delivering the information has by far the greatest impact on the audience.

Verbal Presentation

The basis of all presentations is content. The content is what draws the audience to the presentation. Even though it is clear that the specific words you say as part of presentations may be less memorable than the images and impressions you create, without effective content you literally have nothing to say. Your topic must have meaning for your audience. Sometimes the meaning is decided for you, as when you are called to give an update to your superiors on a project; other times you are selecting the topic. Keep your topic focused to sustain your audience's interest. For example, "Going Green" is a wide and somewhat intangible topic. A cost/benefit analysis of switching from serving commercially bottled water in disposable packaging to serving house-purified water in reusable bottles is a much narrower topic with focused and implementable solutions.

However you have arrived at your topic, you need to become an authority on it. Research your topic by reading and speaking with experts. Seek to understand the facts that both support and oppose your view. Your audience will have questions and may challenge your contentions. These are good things, indicating that you have stimulated thought. Be ready for the discussion to veer outside of your particular point of view.

Once you have identified your topic, identify your audience. Is this a project update to department heads? A sales pitch to a potential client? A tasting of the new menu rollout for the front-of-the-house staff? A workshop or lecture to a large group?

Mold your topic toward the intended audience. Will this be a large or small audience? Why do they want to see your presentation? Are you seeking to convey information, encourage collaborative thought, or persuade the audience to embrace your point of view? Consider the demographic of your audience. Are they above, below, or at a similar career level to you? Are they in your field? Are they older, younger, or of similar age to you? What is their presumed level of knowledge of the subject matter? What are their expectations for the subject matter?

Identify the location of the presentation. Understand the layout and electronic capabilities (presentation hardware, hard-line or Wi-Fi Internet access, audio equipment, lighting, and so on). Arrive early to get a feel for the space and to ensure that any presentation materials work.

Create content and materials to fit your topic, the audience, and the space. All three items need to be considered. A multimedia PowerPoint presentation will not work for an intimate audience, in a small room, with no projection technology. Likewise, flip charts and posters are not optimal visual aids in a large room. A demonstration on making pizza will be completely different for college-level culinary students learning Italian cooking versus parents taking a class to learn how to create healthy meals for young children.

Remember that your visual materials (slides, charts, and so on) are supplements and enhancements to your message. Reading content directly from a slide does not engage the audience. It decreases your credibility — the slide, rather than you, becomes the authority.

Vocal Presentation

Recall for a minute Ben Stein's portrayal of the economics teacher in *Ferris Bueller's Day Off*. His pitch and tone never waver, giving the overall effect of listening to white noise. It is easy to identify a similar person in your own life — someone who is very well-informed and has great ideas but whose manner of speaking lulls you to sleep before you can process those ideas. Equally distracting are loud talkers and quiet talkers, those who insert verbal placeholders "like" and "um," those who speak too quickly, and those with a singsong quality to their voices. These and other vocal habits will distract an audience by shifting their focus from your message to how you are delivering your message.

The first step in training yourself to speak more effectively is to listen to yourself speaking. Record yourself when speaking on the phone or during a meeting. The challenge when reviewing the recording is to overcome the common feeling of "I hate listening to myself." We sound different to ourselves than we do to others. Have a trusted friend or mentor listen along to help you identify the differences between your self-prejudice and any vocal qualities that may be impeding your message. As you do this recording-listening exercise several times, you will become accustomed to the sound of your voice and be able to more clearly distinguish the patterns in your speech. Recall your emotional state as well. Listen for how you sound when you are relaxed and well prepared, when you are challenged, and when you challenge another. What happens to your voice when you are referencing visual aids such as slides, charts, or handouts?

You will undoubtedly practice your presentation multiple times before going live. Record these sessions as well. Of course, speaking to a recorder is a world away from speaking in front of an audience, regardless of the size

*A*ltering the tone, cadence, and volume of your voice, intentionally or unintentionally, affects the audience's perception of your message. Consider the effects of speaking consistently in the following ways:

o   Speaking too quickly indicates nervousness and does not allow the audience time to process your information. It also can create distrust — think of the stereotypical slick, fast-speaking salesperson who is trying to get you to say "yes" without paying attention to the details.

o   Speaking too slowly can put your audience to sleep or give the perception that you are talking down to the audience.

o   Speaking too softly will frustrate the portion of the audience who cannot hear you and will

undermine your credibility by indicating that you do not have confidence in your message.

o   Speaking too loudly sends the message that you are yelling.

However, these mannerisms create emphasis when used sparingly and purposefully in conjunction with your normal speaking voice:

o   Speaking slowly in a lower tone indicates seriousness.

o   Speaking quickly in a higher tone shows excitement and joy.

o   Speaking softly draws an audience in, as if listening to a secret.

o   Speaking loudly immediately captures the audience's attention.

of that audience. When live, you will most likely begin to fall back into your normal mode of speaking. Build reminders into your notes to pause, change the pitch of your voice, and avoid saying "um."

The pause is an effective tool for a speaker, and it may be one of the more difficult tools to master. Many of us feel uncomfortable speaking in front of others, and the discomfort grows exponentially when we are not saying anything and the audience is staring back. You may be well rehearsed; however, this stare gives you just the slightest worry that you have forgotten your lines, and that minute doubt begins to throw off your whole game.

Yes, everyone in the audience will be looking at you because you have situated yourself in front of them. Yes, they will be waiting for you to say something because they are in attendance to hear you speak. The truth is that the audience needs a pause. It provides everyone with the time to process the information you have given. It lets them take notes and formulate questions. For instance, during a preservice meeting, the chef should remain silent while the service staff tastes the specials so that they can concentrate on the flavors and consider how they might describe and sell the dish to the guest. A pause allows your audience to understand that you are moving from one topic to another. It also emphasizes that what you have just said is important. There is a limit to how much information anyone can process at a given time. Think about phone numbers. They are not presented as a whole: 8454529600, but rather as segments: 845-452-9600. Build intentional pauses into your presentation. Your message will be more easily received.

Visual Presentation

Audience members will take their cues about how to react to the information from the presenter. Regardless of the presentation's content, the presenter is looked upon as the expert in the room. No matter how you are feeling inside, as a presenter you must come across as a calm, collected, and controlled authority.

Dress is an important consideration, and audience expectations should be taken into account. Watch the President of the United States. When speaking from the White House, he is in a suit, behind a desk or podium, demonstrating that he is "in charge." When he is out with "the people" he has no tie, often no sport coat, and his sleeves are rolled up. In each instance, he is using his dress in a specific, calculated way to enhance his audience's ability to understand and accept his message. Similarly, when presenting a business plan to potential investors, you would be best served by dressing in business attire to instill confidence that investors' money would be utilized wisely, and when performing a cooking demo, you would be best served by wearing clean, pressed chef's whites.

Movement has an impact on your message. Too little movement, such as presenting to a live audience from behind a podium, can be as distracting as continual pacing across a stage. An audience will be most at ease when you are moving naturally. Make a point or two standing in one place, so the audience can focus on your message, not your movement. During a natural pause, move to a different location to make your next point. The movement will help to maintain your audience's visual attention.

Strive to be balanced in your posture. Slouching, leaning, and sitting may translate into signs of indifference or weakness, undermining your position as an expert. Excess rigidity can seem too authoritative, as if you are speaking at, not with, your audience. Use gestures as visual punctuation to provide emphasis to your point. Keep your hands out of your pockets. If you know this is a habit, be sure to empty your pockets before beginning your presentation. This may reduce your tendency to fiddle with these items, and it will reduce any noise disturbances caused by rattling keys, change, or other items.

The audience will take many cues about how to react to your presentation from your facial expression. Practice using facial expressions to emphasize your message, either in front of a mirror or by recording and watching yourself. Display compassion, excitement, authority, anger, sadness, joy, and other emotions as they are appropriate to your message.

In order to effectively use your expression to influence your audience, you must face the people. Turning away from them breaks the connection you have created. Any time you turn, use audiovisual aids, or gesture, keep your face in view of the audience members and your body turned toward them. Focusing on maintaining eye contact will assist you with this. The Latitude Learning Center's seminar "Giving an Effective Presentation" takes eye contact one step further into what they call "Eye Communication." The presenter makes eye contact with individuals in the audience for three to five seconds as opposed to just scanning the audience. This creates a direct connection, echoing the feeling of a one-on-one conversation. Select audience members at random rather than moving in a predictable pattern. The audience will quickly adjust to a predictable pattern, and the effect will be lost.

Involve Your Audience

Effective presentations involve the audience. The attention of audience members will not be long maintained if they are asked to sit in one spot and look in the same place for an extended length of time, no matter how important or interesting the material. Create an opportunity for the audience to give feedback and ask questions. Aside from benefiting the audience, it provides you with the opportunity to ensure that your audience is understanding your message correctly. An educator may demonstrate a technique in stages, allowing students to practice as they go rather than having to attempt to remember all of the details of something new at one time. Similarly, when training a new employee, the trainer can demonstrate one task and then ask the new hire to complete the same task right away. Create audience-driven segments in which the audience can break into groups and apply or practice the information you are presenting. Let the groups provide feedback to the entire audience. Use humor to let the audience express emotion out loud. Use audiovisual aids which incorporate movement, color, and sound.

Make the Audience Comfortable

The physical environment of the room will influence your audience and affect people's ability to receive your message.

- *Adjust the temperature. Sweating and shivering alike will distract the audience.*

- *Do a sound check and test any audiovisual aids before the audience arrives.*

- *Consider having pens and paper available for audience members to take notes if they wish.*

- *Ask the audience to silence cell phones.*

- *The option of food and drink attracts people and makes them comfortable. If coffee is offered, have decaf available. Any snacks should be handheld and create minimal mess and noise.*

- *Providing something to drink is a benefit, but it also necessitates bathroom breaks. Plan for brief breaks throughout your presentation, and let the audience know when they will be in advance.*

Just as your writing improves through reading and your cooking improves through eating, your presentation skills improve by watching and copying those who are skilled at presenting. Some of the best speakers in the world participate in TED talks, online lectures on a range of topics available on TED's Web site.

Meetings

Meetings are a special category of presentation. Increase in position generally dictates increased time spent in and conducting meetings. Work is accomplished in meetings — that is, if the meetings are planned, coordinated, and conducted with this goal in mind. **To make your meetings do more work, consider the following:**

○ *Determine the purpose of the meeting. Write down exactly what you are hoping to accomplish. You will be sharing this purpose with others.*

○ *Based on the purpose, determine if holding a meeting is the most effective option.*

○ *Decide who needs to be in attendance and how much time the meeting will take. Resist the urge to involve everyone all of the time.*

○ *Create a time and place and send an invitation through e-mail. Let the attendees know the purpose for the meeting. Ask for an RSVP. If your company has a shared calendar function, perform a busy search rather than ask for input on date and time. As the person calling the meeting, you are in control. Much time will be wasted with back-and-forth e-mails asking attendees to collectively determine a convenient time.*

○ *Create an agenda, breaking the meeting down into topics, presenters, and length of time devoted to both. Distribute this to the attendees in advance.*

○ *If information needs to be reviewed by the attendees prior to the meeting, ensure that it is distributed. Ensure that you have read, researched, and planned accordingly.*

○ *During the meeting, control the flow. Keep to topic and keep to time. Assign someone to take minutes. If questions or tangents arise that do not fit within the allotted time, follow up after the meeting. If further action is needed, assign specific duties to specific attendees.*

○ *Following the meeting, send a thank-you note to the attendees outlining any further action and the owner of that action, if appropriate. Send the minutes and any audiovisual items used (such as slide shows) as soon as possible.*

Running effective meetings

Video Presentations and Social Media

In a digital age, utilizing various media to promote yourself and your employer is not an option — it is an essential element of success. Your decisions regarding what content to promote and which platforms are best suited to your needs must be driven by carefully defined goals. Social media and blogs are wonderful, free tools that allow you to connect and interact with others, establish yourself as an authority, and vicariously monitor what others are saying regarding a specific topic. A third element that is widely accessible with little investment is video.

Presenting via video involves many of the same considerations as presenting in front of a live audience: adjusting the message to fit the audience and paying attention to verbal, vocal, and visual cues and qualities. **Some considerations that are unique to video are as follows:**

- ○ **Timing.** *Watch videos on similar topics and notice when your attention begins to wander. Study morning news shows. Notice that the segments run from one-and-a-half minutes to three minutes. Short format works best. If cooking, break down the recipe into workable segments adjusted for your audience. A twelve-hour braising video will not hold an audience's attention.*

- ○ **Feedback.** *You will not have the immediate feedback loop that is present with a live audience. In person, if you see yawning, you can immediately adjust. On video, if the audience becomes bored, they navigate away. Before posting your video, ask several people to watch and critique it.*

- ○ **Cinematography.** *Pay close attention to camerawork. One steady straight shot becomes very boring very quickly; unsteady shots are distracting and appear amateurish. Show your face, and smile. After all, you are the expert. Pay attention to lighting and sound. The frame should appear naturally lit, and the speaker should use a normal speaking voice.*

Remember that video may reach a much wider audience than a live presentation. Use universal terms rather than industry jargon to make the video meaningful to those who are interested but not professionals. Video is a marketing tool, not a doctoral dissertation. How can video be effective for you? **Here are some examples:**

- ○ *Demonstrate a technique.*

- ○ *Showcase a signature dish.*

- ○ *Introduce or explain a topic.*

- ○ *Advertise an upcoming presentation, a product, or a service.*

- ○ *Apply for a new position with a video résumé.*

- ○ *Train staff.*

○ *Share a weekly, monthly, or quarterly update with customers, clients, and/or staff.*

Whatever the reason, remember that videos must enhance and be aligned with your individual message. If posted to an open forum, they become searchable, they have the potential to reach a wide audience, and they do not go away.

Giving Back: Becoming a Mentor

"Mentor: someone whose hindsight can become your foresight." — Chinese proverb

Earlier in this work we discussed having a mentor as being one of the foundational tools of your career. Thus far in your career, you may have considered the mentor relationship only from the point of view of someone being mentored. Indeed, seeking counsel from a trusted advisor who has traversed the path you are currently walking, faced the challenges you are facing, and has been called upon to make similar difficult decisions to the ones you are making can be of great benefit throughout your career. It is natural that as your career grows, others will seek your advice about their careers.

Becoming a mentor can occur organically. You develop a professional relationship with someone who is in an earlier career stage than you are, and that relationship grows and becomes sustained over an extended period of time. You may have this type of relationship with many individuals without labeling yourself as one person's "mentor." There are also opportunities for a more formal, structured mentor-mentee relationship. Many schools offer formal mentorship programs that seek to connect students with alumni; professional organizations connect novices with experienced professionals; and some employers connect new hires with tenured employees.

Why would you want to become a mentor? Aren't there enough challenges in and outside of work at this point in your life and career? You may find that you are at a point in your career when you would like to give something back, in the same way that others gave of themselves to you. Perhaps you identify raw talent in an individual and feel you can help cultivate that potential into success. Similarly, you may notice a troubled individual who will benefit from structure and guidance. After all, no matter the details of your current position, you are in the hospitality industry, and something in your nature encourages you to help others.

The twin foundations of a mentor-mentee relationship are trust and communication. You must demonstrate through your own actions that you are trustworthy, professional, and informed, and that you make good decisions. This is an intimate relationship; when people seek advice they are in a vulnerable place, having admitted to themselves and another that they do not know something, or are having difficulty making a decision. Even if you never break the trust of your mentee, if that person sees that you have broken another's trust or are acting contrary to how you are advising him or her to act, you will have hurt the relationship.

Open communication comes from and builds trust. Questions and opportunities arise at unpredictable times. Often those early in their careers may feel uneasy about asking questions. They may feel that the questions are stupid, because the answers or reasons seem obvious to others. They may have been discouraged from asking questions by inhospitable superiors in the past. They may not want to admit any weakness for fear of losing face. Create an environment where a mentee can ask any question, without worry or fear of repercussion. Be willing to answer all questions, from very basic to very complex, to the best of your ability and with the mind of an educator. Also, be willing to say, "I don't know, but I'll find out." You do not have to have all the answers, nor are you expected to shoulder all of the responsibility of a mentee's development. You just have to care, and let your mentee know that you care.

Being a mentor is a highly individualized relationship. Formal mentor programs will likely have specified check-ins and documentation that needs to be submitted; even so, the actual relationship will vary greatly between individuals. As a seasoned professional, you have developed the ability to assess an individual and adjust your communication toward that person according to his or her capacity to receive your message. Recognize that some need more communication and assurance, and some need less. Some can handle frank commentary and criticism, while others benefit best from a softer approach.

It is important to establish boundaries with this relationship. You are not on call 24/7, you are not taking responsibility to ensure your mentee will get all he or she is after, nor are you there to always agree with your protégé's ideas and actions. A mentor is a balance of sounding board, cheerleader, and voice of reason. Assure your mentee that you are there to provide assistance, but he or she must make the appropriate decision after considering your input. It is okay to challenge your mentee to figure it out, whatever "it" may be. This is a valuable gift. Having the opportunity to figure something out and to succeed or fail on your own merit, rather than just being given direction, is a sign of progression. You are demonstrating that you have the confidence in your mentee's ability and capability to make his or her own decisions. Of course, you will provide encouragement and feedback, but never judgment.

Whether the relationship is formal or informal, some structure will assist with keeping the relationship active, relevant, and enriching for both mentor and mentee.

- ○ **Schedule check-ins.** *This can be as simple as tagging your calendar quarterly to give your mentee a call. Let the person know you are interested and available.*

- ○ **Have a conversation about goals and history.** *Understand the mentee's progression thus far and where he or she is looking to go. Ask periodically for an updated résumé.*

- ○ **Check-in informally.** *Forward an interesting article or Web site link. Let your protégé know about job opportunities, and introduce him or her to your contacts.*

- ○ **Give your mentee "homework":** *some tangible, measurable item to be accountable for between formal meetings.*

- ○ **Tell your contacts about the strengths of your mentee** — *not to boost your own ego, but to promote the success of someone who deserves it.*

Summary

"Master" is not a designation based on age or career length. Rather, the stage of master indicates the achievement of a high degree of knowledge and skill; contributions that direct an organization; the creation of intellectual property that moves the profession forward; and a willingness to share and return the gift of assistance you once received (and may continue to receive) by mentoring novices and journeymen as their own career trees grow. Even though you have gained so much throughout your career, continue to cultivate the ability to think of your career in the same way you did when you were starting out: There are endless possibilities, and by setting goals and systematically working to achieve them, you can turn dreams into realities. As the Zen proverb says: "When you get to the top of the mountain, keep climbing."

Exercise

Keep Climbing

By virtue of reaching the master stage of your career, you have proven that you can create and achieve goals; build, maintain, and utilize a network; articulately and persuasively present yourself to employers, clients, and staff; and deliver results at a high level. In short, you have reached the long-term goals you set earlier in your career. Return to the beginning of the process and create new short-term, intermediate, and long-term goals for a new project. This could be a new professional aspiration within your current area of expertise or a completely new venture. This could be a hobby, or an area/topic of interest that you would like to learn more about. This could be your dream retirement plan. Whatever it may be, keep challenging yourself to grow.

Appendix 1

SALARIES IN THE CULINARY INDUSTRY

The average annual salaries for some culinary careers are listed below.

JOB TITLE	AVERAGE ANNUAL SALARY
Chef	$41,575
Pastry Chef	$36,848
Manager	$36,798

(Figures from www.foodservice.com)

Your salary can increase or decrease based on a combination of many factors, one of which is education. The level of education and the degrees that you possess can make a big difference in terms of what you will get paid. The figures below are general numbers that apply across all industries.

LEVEL OF EDUCATION ACHIEVED	AVERAGE ANNUAL SALARY
No high school diploma	$20,110
High school graduate	$28,307
Associate Degree	$36,392
Bachelor's Degree	$50,056
Master's Degree	$63,220

(Figures from U.S. Census Bureau 1998 data)

In addition to your education, another factor that affects salaries is the volume of sales in a given establishment.

JOB TITLE	ANNUAL SALARY RANGE		
Operations with Annual Gross Income Under $1,499,999			
	LOW	AVERAGE	HIGH
General Manager	$30,000	$39,000	$48,000
Front-of-House Manager	$26,000	$33,000	$40,000
Executive Chef	$29,000	$37,000	$45,000
Sous Chef/Kitchen Manager	$26,000	$32,000	$38,000
Operations with Annual Gross Income of $1,500,000 to 2,999,999			
	LOW	AVERAGE	HIGH
General Manager	$36,000	$47,000	$58,000
Front-of-House Manager	$30,000	$38,000	$46,000
Executive Chef	$34,000	$49,500	$65,000
Sous Chef/Kitchen Manager	$30,000	$36,500	$43,000
Operations with Annual Gross Income of $3,000,000 to 4,999,999			
	LOW	AVERAGE	HIGH
General Manager	$44,000	$57,000	$70,000
Front-of-House Manager	$36,000	$45,000	$54,000
Executive Chef	$40,000	$52,500	$65,000
Sous Chef/Kitchen Manager	$34,000	$41,000	$48,000

JOB TITLE	ANNUAL SALARY RANGE		
Operations with Annual Gross Income of $5,000,000 to 9,999,999			
	LOW	AVERAGE	HIGH
General Manager	$52,000	$67,000	$82,000
Front-of-House Manager	$44,000	$54,000	$64,000
Executive Chef	$48,000	$64,000	$80,000
Sous Chef/Kitchen Manager	$40,000	$47,500	$55,000
Operations with Annual Gross Income of $10,000,000+			
	LOW	AVERAGE	HIGH
General Manager	$62,000	$79,000	$96,000
Front-of-House Manager	$52,000	$64,000	$76,000
Executive Chef	$58,000	$69,000	$80,000
Sous Chef/Kitchen Manager	$46,000	$55,500	$65,000

Appendix II

JOB OUTLOOK AND SALARIES FOR SPECIFIC JOBS AND CAREERS IN THE CULINARY ARTS

Cooks and Food Preparation Workers

These individuals are responsible for the day-to-day cooking and preparation of food. The Bureau of Labor Statistics (BLS) categorizes cooks as those who follow recipes to completion and food preparation workers as those who perform repetitive tasks and prepare ingredients for complex recipes. These workers stand for long periods, lift heavy objects, and work in high-heat and high-humidity environments. Workers may have been trained on the job or have vocational, trade school, or other post-secondary training (apprenticeships).

○ *30 million total workers.*

○ *35 percent of workers are below 24 years old, and about one-third are part-time.*

○ *Two-thirds of workers are employed by restaurants and full-service eating and drinking establishments, 16 percent by institutions such as schools, hospitals, nursing care, and the balance by grocery stores and hotels.*

○ *Outlook is good through 2018, but with slower than average growth.*

Restaurant Cooks

- *Median: $21,990; Lowest 10 percent: $15,880; Middle 50 percent: $18,230–$26,150; Highest 10 percent: $31,330.*

Food Preparation Workers

- *Median: $18,630; lowest 10 percent: $14,730; middle 50 percent: $16,180–$22,500; highest 10 percent: $27,440.*

Private Household Cooks

- *Median: $24,070; lowest 10 percent: $16,230; middle 50 percent: $19,030–$36,590; highest 10 percent: $56,280.*

Institutional and Café Cooks

- *Median: $22,210; lowest 10 percent: $15, 220; middle 50 percent: $17,850–27,460; highest 10 percent: 33,050*

Chefs, Head Cooks, Food Preparation and Serving Supervisors

These individuals oversee the daily operations of foodservice operations, including restaurants, hotels, institutional and volume service, and catering businesses. Chefs and head cooks oversee the kitchen staff and are the most highly skilled cooks; food preparation and serving supervisors oversee both kitchen and non kitchen staff. In addition to the actual preparation and service of food, individuals in these roles hire and train staff and are responsible for inventory, ordering, creating workflow lists, and ensuring that the operation runs smoothly, meets health code standards, and is profitable.

These individuals have extensive experience. Some may have formal training (two- or four-year college degree), and some may have been promoted to the position with little or no formal education.

- *941,600 workers.*

- *Expected 6 percent growth between 2008 and 2018, which is slower than average.*

- *Prospects are good, with tougher competition for positions in upscale environments. Candidates with good business sense have better prospects.*

- *Median salary: $38,770; lowest 10 percent: $22,120; middle 50 percent: $29,050–$51,540; highest 10 percent: $66,680.*

Chefs and Head Cooks

Chef's and head cooks make up about 12 percent of the workers in this general category.

- *50 percent of all chefs and head cooks work in full-service establishments; 9 percent work in hotels, 9 percent as caterers, 9 percent in contract service, and 8 percent are self-employed.*

Food Preparation and Serving Supervisors

Food preparation and serving supervisors make up about 88 percent of the workers in this general category.

- *43 percent work in limited service operations, 25 percent in full-service operations.*

Foodservice Managers

Managers are responsible for the daily operations of the establishment. They coordinate with different departments, perform administrative functions (budgeting, inventory, ordering, and so on), and recruit, hire, and train staff. They are called upon to resolve guest complaints and resolve conflict between staff members.

Many managers have a two- or four-year college degree, and many companies require candidates to successfully complete formal training programs. Managers are the face of the establishment, ensuring that all organizational standards are met.

- *5 percent growth between 2008 and 2018, which is slower than average.*

- ○ *Prospects are good, with high levels of competition for upscale locations.*

- ○ *Median: $46,320; lowest 10 percent: $29,450; middle 50 percent: $36,670–$59,580; highest 10 percent: $76,940.*

Food and Beverage Service and Related Workers

These individuals interact directly with customers and guests. They are standing the majority of the time, and they carry heavy objects. Training is typically provided on the job.

- ○ *7.7 million workers; 21 percent are between 16 and 19 years old.*

- ○ *There are abundant openings, with above average growth expected.*

Wages are generally hourly, and may be a combination of hourly wage and tips. **Hourly salaries for food preparation and serving (including fast food) are as follows:**

- ○ *Median: $7.90; lowest 10 percent: $6.67; middle 50 percent: $7.26–$9.12; highest 10 percent: $10.67.*

Waitstaff

- ○ *Median: $8.01; lowest 10 percent: $6.73; middle 50 percent: $7.32–$10.35; highest 10 percent: $14.26.*

Bartenders

○ *Median: $8.54; lowest 10 percent: $8.54; middle 50 percent: $7.53–$10.98; highest 10 percent: $14.93.*

Hosts

○ *Median: $8.42; lowest 10 percent: $6.88; middle 50 percent: $7.50–$9.70; highest 10 percent: $11.89.*

Dishwashers

○ *Median: $8.19; lowest 10 percent: $6.90; middle 50 percent: $7.47–$9.35; highest 10 percent: $10.74.*

Top Executives

These are the top-level positions. These individuals are responsible for crafting organizational goals and policies and the strategies for meeting and implementing them. These positions require extensive experience and bachelor- or master-level degrees (or higher).

Little to no change in job growth is expected, as these tend to be long-term positions.

○ *Median: $91,570; middle 50 percent: $62,900–$137,020.*

○ *Earnings can vary greatly due to company size. Benefits packages, including stock options and bonuses, are also factored into the total compensation package.*

Food Communications: Writers, Editors, Photographers, and Stylists

Food communication is the coverage of culinary topics in newspapers, magazines, and books and on radio, television, and the Internet.

Food writers are communicators with a good basic knowledge of food and cooking. Some food writers edit or write books. There is a huge market for food books on every imaginable subject.

Food writers also submit articles to magazines and newspapers. To write these articles, you need to be well-read in the culinary arts and proficient in the kitchen. Articles could range from a simple discussion of how to brew a pot of tea to an informational piece on nutritional cooking.

Restaurant critics are food writers who understand what good food, good cooking, and good service is all about. They are able to discuss the style of a restaurant and trends in the restaurant business. Restaurant critics are very important to restaurants, especially when their good reviews increase business.

Food photographers have the talent of making food look visually appealing in print. You see their work in ad campaigns and magazines and on book jackets. Their challenge is to photograph food so the viewer can almost taste it. What's required is an understanding of photography and lighting.

Food stylists work with food photographers. They are responsible for preparing and placing the food just right on the plate. Their culinary knowledge is critical — how to select the best product, apply the right technique, and cut the item expertly. It is up to the stylist to make sure that the lettuce leaves are perfect, with not a single blemish, and the entire presentation is picture-perfect.

Requirements

Culinary and writing skills (food writers and critics), culinary skills and knowledge of photography and design (food photographers and stylists).

Helpful to Have

Broad knowledge of the food industry and all food media outlets.

Salary Ranges

○ *$20,000–$55,000+. Many jobs are freelance, paid on a per project, hourly, or per diem basis. Salaries can be higher depending on region.*

Research and Development

Food scientists and technologists use their knowledge of chemistry, physics, engineering, microbiology, biotechnology, sensory sciences, and consumer behavior and other sciences to develop new or better ways of preserving, processing, packaging, storing, and delivering foods. Some food scientists engage in basic research, such as discovering new food sources; analyzing food content; or searching for substitutes for harmful or undesirable additives such as nitrites. Some research improvements in traditional food-processing techniques, such as baking, blanching, canning, drying, evaporation, and pasteurization. Others enforce government regulations, inspecting food-processing areas and ensuring that sanitation, safety, quality, and waste-management standards are met.

Food technologists generally work in product development, applying the findings from food science research to improve the selection, preservation, processing, packaging, and distribution of foods. They also work to improve the nutritional value of foods and menus offered to consumers.

Entry-Level Requirements

At entry level, a Bachelor of Science degree with course work in food chemistry, food and nutrient analysis, food engineering, and microbiology. Although many individuals entering the area of food science have a predominantly science background, an increasing number arrive with culinary arts degrees or experience, as well as degrees related specifically to food science and technology.

Helpful for Advancement

To move up into areas of research and development as a manager, you will need advanced degrees (either a master's degree in an area of science or a PhD in food science or related areas such as biology, chemistry, or nutrition).

Salary Ranges

○ **Lab assistant:** *$30,000–$60,000.*

○ **Team leader or lab manager:** *$35,000–$80,000.*

○ **Director:** *$90,000+ (PhD is typically required at this level).*

Test Kitchen and Recipe Development

Test kitchen researchers help major food companies, restaurant chains, and specialty food producers develop new products. Using their culinary skills in professional test kitchens, researchers analyze how the product acts when it is heated, refrigerated, stored on a shelf, or frozen. Test kitchen professionals must be organized, methodical, and scientific in their approach to their work.

Test kitchen recipe developers typically work at food magazines or they are free-lance writers who prepare recipes as part of the articles they write. They must be able to develop recipes that will showcase the flavor, texture, color, and/or nutritional characteristic of a particular food. Recipe developers must research the food and write about it in a way that will be useful for the home or professional cook. This work may also offer an opportunity to break into the world of food styling and even food photography.

Recipe testers are hired by cookbook authors to check recipes before publication. Magazines and newspapers also hire recipe testers to work in-house on recipes for publication.

To break into this work, you can write to publishing houses that have produced cookbooks you admire. Or, you can read trade journals that might have information about who is working on a cookbook, and then write directly to the author to find out if he or she is looking for help testing recipes.

Recipe testers are paid a flat fee per recipe and are reimbursed for the food items purchased to prepare the recipes.

Requirements

Culinary degree and organizational skills (test kitchen researchers), culinary and writing skills (test kitchen recipe developers), culinary skills (recipe testers).

Helpful to Have

Knowledge of marketing (test kitchen researchers).

Salary Ranges

○   **Test kitchen professionals:** *$20,000–$55,000+.*

○   **Recipe testers:** *Compensation is typically paid per recipe and varies.*

Appendix III

QUESTIONS IN THE INTERVIEW

Questions Asked by Employers

The following questions are frequently asked by employers. Some are general, others come directly from employers who have attended our Career Fairs. When thinking about answers, remember that employers like specifics. Although you will not be able to plan for every possible question, knowing yourself and knowing the potential employer will help you to respond to every question with confidence.

Education

○ *Why did you choose your school?*

○ *What was your favorite class?*

○ *Who was your favorite instructor and why?*

○ *How do you feel that your education has prepared you for this job?*

○ *What leadership roles did you take on while a student?*

○ *What outside activities did you participate in?*

- Do your grades reflect your abilities?

  _____

- What were some defining moments in your education?

  _____

- Do you plan on returning to school to continue your education? What subject?

  _____

- What changes would you make to the current school program?

  _____

- Where did you do your externship, and what did you like/dislike about the experience?

  _____

Experience

  _____

- Why did you leave your last job?

  _____

- What motivates you at work?

  _____

- How would your last supervisor describe you?

  _____

- What did you like most/least about your last position or supervisor?

  _____

- Tell me about a time you had a conflict with someone at work and how it was resolved.

  _____

- Tell me about a team or individual project you have worked on.

  _____

- What skills have you acquired that will help you to succeed in this job?

  _____

- Why are you looking to change jobs?

  _____

- Tell me about a time when you displayed excellent customer service.

  _____

- *Have you ever been terminated?*

- *Do you have any regrets about how you left a former position?*

- *Tell me about a time when you did something outside your job description.*

- *Tell me about a review you had with either a supervisor or instructor. How did you react to their suggestions?*

- *Tell me about some of your recent goals and how you achieved them.*

- *Do you do something at work (or school) better than anyone else?*

- *Tell me about a time when you had to work under a deadline.*

- *You have VIPs coming in. You have access to any ingredients and ample time to prepare. What would you make and why?*

- *What do you like about serving the public?*

- *Give an example of a time when you provided a solution to a supervisor.*

- *How did your last position relate to the success of the company?*

- *Would you be available to stage?*

- *Basic culinary knowledge, such as: Describe the steps to braising. Describe the creaming method. What is the correct holding temperature for raw eggs? What does the term pincage mean? What is the size of small dice? What is the ratio for a pie crust?*

Personal

- *Why do you want to work here?*

- *What do you know about us?*

- *Where do you want to be in five years?*

- *What are some of your goals and how do you plan to achieve them?*

- *What are your strengths?*

- *What are your weaknesses?*

- *Why did you get into this industry?*

- *What does it mean to you to be a "chef"?*

- *Do your co-workers/classmates consider you a leader?*

- *What are the three most important values you hold?*

- *What is your biggest accomplishment?*

- *What are the top three reasons why you take a job?*

- *What do you think you could bring to this job?*

- *What are your hobbies or interests?*

- *Define success. Define failure.*

- *Have you had any failures, and what did you learn from them?*

- *You have just won the lottery and never have to work again. What would you do with the winnings?*

- *Do you plan on obtaining any professional certifications?*

- *Describe your ideal job.*

- *Do you prefer working alone or with a team?*

- *How do you feel about relocating?*

- *What do you like the least about working in the restaurant business?*

- *If you could go back, what is one change you would make about a past decision?*

- *Why should I hire you over the other candidates?*

- *What is not on your résumé that you would like to tell me?*

- *What qualities should a successful manager possess?*

- *Tell me about a time that you assisted someone.*

- *What is your management style?*

- *Do you have any questions for me?*

Oddities

These questions are more about testing your ability to think on your feet than they are about obtaining accurate information.

○ *Tell me a joke.*

○ *How many gas stations are there in LA?*

○ *If you could have dinner with anybody, who would it be?*

○ *What kind of music do you listen to?*

Questions to Ask Potential Employers

Interviewing is a two-way street. In order to make a decision about a position, it is important to have all the facts. Interviewers look highly upon candidates who ask questions — it demonstrates that a candidate is prepared, and past performance is an indicator of future performance. You may write these questions down, and you should feel free to take some notes on the answers.

○ *Please describe the duties of the job.*

○ *Describe a typical day or week.*

○ *Is there a potential for rotation, and through which stations?*

○ *Who will be my supervisor?*

○ *How are the day-to-day assignments communicated?*

○ *How will my performance be evaluated, and how often?*

- *What is the potential for advancement?*

- *Does this position have any input for specials or menu items?*

- *How often does the menu change?*

- *How have you kept up with industry trends?*

- *What plans does the company have for growth over the next year?*

- *How long have you been with the company?*

- *What attracted you to this company/position?*

- *Do you promote from within?*

- *How long has the management team worked together?*

- *Has there been much turnover with this position?*

- *May I speak with the person who is in this position?*

- *What traits are you looking for in the person you will hire?*

- *Describe a "successful" employee.*

- *Would I need to supply my own equipment and uniforms?*

- *Do you provide housing?*

- *Describe a typical customer.*

- *If a customer has a complaint, what is the company's procedure for addressing the issue?*

○ Are there opportunities for outside projects (competitions, off-site catering, and so on)?

_____

○ How much of the products are made in-house?

_____

○ How often do you receive meat, produce, and fish?

_____

○ Which vendors do you currently use?

_____

○ How many people do you serve on an average weekday? Weekend?

_____

○ What is the average cost of an entrée?

_____

○ Do you belong to any professional organizations?

_____

○ How many employees are there in the kitchen?

_____

○ What are the best-selling items in each category?

_____

○ What do you do to attract new customers?

_____

○ What encourages a customer to return?

_____

○ If an employee makes a mistake, describe for me what would happen.

_____

○ What is your background?

_____

○ What is the best/worst thing about your job? The company?

_____

○ What is your management style?

_____

○ How would your employees describe you?

_____

○ Who was influential in your career?

_____

○ What is the next step? (Set up the next point of contact.)

_____

Appendix IV

JOB SEARCH AND PROFESSIONAL DEVELOPMENT RESOURCES

General Job Search

There are a number of Web sites devoted to job searches. General job listing sites will include jobs in virtually any industry and for any level of skill. Often, you can apply for a posted job directly through the Web site, but you will need to have an electronic version of your résumé ready. Some sites will let you post your résumé on their site, which makes it easy to complete online applications and lets employers search for you. You may also be able to sign up for alerts that let you know when jobs that fit your search criteria are posted. For links to some job search sites, visit *www.wiley.com/college/cia*.

You can narrow your search in a number of ways to get the most effective results and see only the jobs that fit your particular requirements. Consider searching by using some of the following:

○ *Location, if you know have a specific geographic preference or restriction*

○ *Salary range*

○ *Position or title, for instance*

    chef   *line cook (saucier, rôtisseur,*
    sous chef   *grillardin, etc.)*
                                    garde manger

pastry chef	butcher
baker	banquet chef
baker's assistant	private chef

For banquet and catering positions, include the following terms along with a title:

banquet	event management
hotel	conference center
resort	school foodservice
catering chef	entertainment foodservice
event planning	contract foodservice

For front-of-the-house positions:

dining room manager	bartender
captain	barista
waiter	sommelier
back waiter	wine steward

For listings that fall outside the traditional restaurant positions, try these terms along with a position title:

ski resort	hospital
spa	magazine
chalet	publishing
yacht	editor
international	research
household manager	test kitchen
government	sales
consulate	research and development
corporate	product development
school	food processing
university	food manufacture

In addition to large job sites, you may also want to find out if a restaurant, company, or corporation that you'd like to work for maintains a Web site and if they post job listings on their site. Some of these jobs may also be posted on general or special intersest Web sites, but some will only be listed on the company's site.

Hospitality Jobs

You can use sites that are specific to the hospitality industry (for links, see *www.wiley.com/college/cia*). Some sites include both job listings and business opportunities. Some are focused on certain segments of the industry, such as clubs or management. To use them effectively, be sure to spend some time getting familiar with the way they organize and post jobs. As you should for general job sites, have electronic versions of your résumé and your cover letter available to make online applications a simple process. If you post your résumé, employers may be able to search for you. Most sites ask that you register, although often registration is free. You can typically narrow your search using the same search terms or keywords that you might on a general Web site. Be sure to sign up for email alerts that can keep you in the loop when new positions are posted.

International Jobs

Finding an international job is essentially the same process as looking for a job in the United States. You can start your search by locating sites devoted to culinary postings overseas by entering the following phrase into a search engine: *international chef job listings*. From there you can search a variety of boards and further narrow your search by country, city, job titles, and more. To narrow your search even further, consider adding terms like these: *catering, hotel, private, cruise, boat,* or *consulate*.

Searching the job listings on multinational corporations such as Hilton, Omni, Nestlé, or Marriott may also yield information about jobs those specific corporations have listed. For links to a sampling of job search sites, visit *www.wiley.com/college/cia*.

Résumé

Since your résumé is such an important tool as you develop your career, you should take advantage of the many resources available, from templates to résumé writing services. Many general job sites offer information about writing effective résumés. Some offer a service that will review and revise your resume, or that will write it for you based upon details you provide. You must typically pay for these services. Visit *www.wiley.com/college/cia* to find links to templates, resources, and more.

Interviews

Many of the general job search sites provide a great deal of additional support and information that can help you to do your best throughout the application and interviewing process. Search on terms such as *job search etiquette, virtual interview, frequently asked interview questions,* or *interview etiquette* to locate these sources.

Recommendation Letters

Your recommendation letters should work to your advantage. To that end, you should devote some energy to planning for them. Many employers, teachers, and community leaders write recommendation letters, but providing these people with some guidance concerning what you specifically would like is a benefit for everyone. Search on line for examples of effective recommendation letters.

Salary

Whether you are preparing for an interview, doing research to find your dream job, or negotiating a salary before starting a new job, you need accurate information about the going rates. You can search government materials, such as those provided by the Bureau of Labor Statistics (BLS), or you can simply search for *culinary salaries. Salary calculators* and *cost of living calculators* are also important tools. For links to some of these resources, visit *www.wiley.com/college/cia.*

Professional Organizations and Resources for Chefs

American Culinary Federation (ACF)

180 Center Place Way
St. Augustine, FL 32095
(800) 624-9458

As the authority on cooking in America since 1929, ACF is the premier professional chefs' organization in North America with more than 20,000 members in more than 200 chapters. From regional and national events to certification and publications, ACF provides resources that will keep chefs and cooks on the cutting edge and involved with the culinary industry. The ACF offers numerous member benefits, as well as administering the certification exams for Certified Master Chef (CMC), and Certified Master Pastry Chef (CMPC).

National Restaurant Association (NRA)

2055 L Street, NW
Washington, DC 20036
(202) 331-5900
(800) 424-5156

National Restaurant Association Educational Foundation (NRAEF)

175 West Jackson Boulevard, Suite 1500
Chicago, IL 60604-2702
(800) 765-2122

Since 1919, the National Restaurant Association (NRA) has worked in coordination with the National Restaurant Association Education Foundation (NRAEF) to lead America's restaurant industry into a new era of prosperity, prominence, and participation. This lobbying organization now represents more than 380,000 businesses from restaurants and suppliers to educators and nonprofits, and provides each one with the valuable resources needed to stay ahead in a fast-paced industry. The organization maintains a Web site with both publicly accessible information (including their job listings), as well as members-only content.

International Association of Culinary Professionals (IACP)

1221 Avenue of the Americas, 42nd Floor
New York, NY 10020
(646) 358-4957
(866) 358-4951

The International Association of Culinary Professionals (IACP) is a world-wide forum for the development and exchange of information, knowledge, and inspiration within the professional food and beverage community. Since first coming together in 1978, IACP has grown to have a multifaceted membership that includes chefs, restaurateurs, foodservice operators, writers, photographers, stylists, marketers, nutritionists, and academia, hailing from hospitality, tourism, publishing, and many other disciplines.

Professional Organizations and Resources for Bakers and Pastry Chefs

American Baker's Association (ABA)

1300 I (Eye) Street NW, Suite 700 West
Washington, DC 20005
(202) 789-0300

Established in 1897, the American Baker's Association (ABA) is an advocacy group located in Washington, DC. They maintain a Web site as a professional baking resource and offer two different types of memberships: bakers and suppliers. Baking and baking R&D positions are listed. Registration and membership are required in order to view job postings.

The Bread Bakers Guild of America

670 West Napa Street, Suite B
Sonoma, CA 95476
(707) 935-1468

The Bread Bakers Guild of America has dedicated itself to advancing the artisan baking profession since it was founded in 1993. The Guild is an educational resource for substantive, accurate information on the craft of making bread.

Retail Bakers of America (RBA)

202 Village Circle Suite #1
Slidell, LA 70458
(985) 643-6504
(800) 638-0924

The Retail Bakers of America (RBA) an association of baking professionals from all over the world offering members the opportunity to share knowledge and resources to enhance business operations through learning opportunities, best practices, networking, and industry communication. They sponsor a yearly conference and offer certifications, such as Certified Master Baker (CMB)

Resources for Food Stylists

The Food Stylist and Food Styling Directory is an online resource for food stylists that allows them to list their services. Postings are organized geographically to make it easier for clients to locate food stylists in their area. A link to this resource can be found at *www.wiley.com/college/cia*.

There may be courses in food styling techniques offered through schools or other organizations. Some may confer Continuing Education Credits. Most stylists learn on the job by working as an assistant to a food stylist or with a food photographer. An important resource for stylists is the International Association of Culinary Professionals (IACP) listed above under Professional Resources for Chefs.

In addition to this organization, many stylists turn to books devoted to the topic, including the following titles:

Food Styling: The Art of Preparing Food for the Camera by Delores Custer, published by John Wiley & Sons, Inc, is a nearly 400-page book that covers the art of food styling as well as the business of being a food stylist. Written by a food stylist with over 30 years of experience working in magazines, books, and advertising, Delores Custer has shared her expertise in dealing with food and discusses the specific challenges of getting foods to behave for the camera.

The Food Stylist's Handbook by Denise Vivaldo, published by Gibbs Smith, aims to educate prospective food stylists about the industry. The book mostly focuses on the business aspects of the industry, such as what is expected at a styling job for a magazine image versus a television cooking show. Vivaldo teaches readers how to write press releases, business plans, and contracts of work.

Resources for Instructors

Certified Hospitality Educator (CHE)

800 N. Magnolia Avenue, Suite 300
Orlando, FL 32803
(407) 999-8100
(800) 349-0299

The award-winning Certified Hospitality Educator (CHE) program is the only professional development opportunity designed for hospitality educators around the world, which strives to help culinary and hospitality educators to strengthen students' critical thinking and motivation to learn, share ideas with their peers, and receive recognition for their teaching abilities from students, colleagues, and the industry. They offer training in a variety of areas of hospitality education, from gaming and guest relations to housekeeping and human resources.

The Chronicle of Higher Education

1255 Twenty-Third Street, NW
Seventh Floor
Washington, DC 20037
(202) 466-1000

The Chronicle of Higher Education is a print and online resource for those involved with or interested in education at post-secondary schools, including community colleges and trade and vocational schools as well as traditional four-year colleges and at the post-graduate level. You can create a free account at their Web site, but some material is considered "premium content" and requires a paid membership. Job listings can be seen without an account or membership. To find jobs in the culinary field, enter the word *culinary* into the search box.

In addition to this journal, you can also research culinary and cooking schools by looking up a directory of cooking or culinary schools on line. From there, you can access the sites for various schools to read their job postings.

International Council on Hotel, Restaurant, and Institutional Education (ICHRIE)

2810 North Parham Road, Suite 230
Richmond, Virginia, 23294
(804) 346-4800

Founded in 1946, the International Council on Hotel, Restaurant, and Institutional Education (ICHRIE) is the global advocate of hospitality and tourism education for schools, colleges, and universities offering programs in hotel and restaurant management, foodservice management, and culinary arts.

In recent years, ICHRIE's focus has expanded and its mission statement has evolved, making it a marketplace for facilitating exchanges of information, ideas, research, products, and services related to education, training, and resource development for the hospitality and tourism industry.

Resources for Personal and Private Chefs

The United States Personal Chef Association (USPCA)

7680 Universal Blvd., Suite 550
Orlando, FL 32819
(800) 995-2138

The USPCA has established guidelines and standards for personal chef services to follow. They also provide training, certification, and support for personal chefs who belong to the association. They have an extensive network in the field. Membership is possible at the professional and student level, with professional members having full access to benefits such as insurance and a job referral service. The organization has chapters in regions and cities throughout the United States.

American Personal & Private Chef Association (APPCA)

4572 Delaware Street
San Diego, CA 92116
(800) 644-8389
(619) 294-2436

The American Personal and Private Chef Association (APPCA) offers a range of services and benefits to their members, including a professional diploma and training, access to local chapters, a subscription to the organization's magazine, *Chef,* and job referrals. They offer listings and referrals for positions in the United States and internationally.

Resources for Research and Development Chefs

Research Chefs Association (RCA)

1100 Johnson Ferry Road, Suite 300
Atlanta, GA 30342
(404) 252-3663

Formed in 1996 by a group of food professionals with a common interest in the challenges facing the profession, the Research Chefs Association (RCA) has rapidly has become the premier source of culinary and technical information for the food industry, with a professionally diverse membership including chefs, food scientists, and others involved in product development, food processing, and manufacture.

Index

C